"A wonderful exposition of the clear differences between Islam and Christianity. While not afraid to be forthright, the authors present the material in a winsome way with a desire to see Muslims won to Christ." —Bruce A. McDowell, coauthor of *Muslims and Christians at the Table*

"A stirring read, this timely book does a thorough job of helping the reader navigate through the fog of religious relativism. While many are interesting in equalizing and downsizing religious claims, the authors have bravely and carefully laid out the distinctive doctrines of Christianity in a helpful and accessible way." —Gregg MacDougall, pastor, Willow Grove, Pennsylvania

"Zaka's passion for Muslim evangelism cannot be expressed more clearly than in this book. His biblical and Reformed understanding of Islam will challenge African-American Bible-believing churches to seriously reach out to the thousands of our own people, young and old, who have left the faith for Islam. Full of Qur'anic and biblical teachings, compared side-by-side, this book is written with truth and grace. It is very rare to find such a book, and I recommend it highly. My own church will use it in reaching out to the nearly twenty thousand Muslims in our area." —Wilbert S. Richardson, pastor, Philadelphia; chairman of the board of the Biblical Institute for Islamic Studies in the USA

"As a minister in the streets, marketplace, homes, and even the mosques, I need help in understanding the truth about Islam. Zaka and Coleman have given me such a practical and discerning tool. Its tables listing excerpts from the Qur'an and Bible are priceless and allow me to begin to understand the Islamic mind so that I can reach my growing Muslim neighbors with the Truth." —Kenneth Wallace, evangelist among Muslims and Jews, Philadelphia

"For those who are ready to biblically love, understand, and evangelize Muslims, this book is a must. Dr. Zaka's many years and experience in Muslim evangelism make him a leading expert in America in this important subject. We will be using this useful tool to better equip our people as we reach out to the large, growing Muslim population in our community." —Luis Centano, American Missionary Fellowship, Philadelphia

"Surely there are sincere Muslims who misunderstand orthodox Christianity's incompatibility with their own essential Islamic precepts. This book will crystallize the radical distinctions between biblical Christianity and Islam that have become murky in popular writings and speeches. I can verify Dr. Zaka's kind regard for Muslims and his earnest desire to allow the Bible to resonate in the hearts of all who, by God's grace, will hear. This fine book contributes enormously toward better understanding." —Robert H. Miller, executive director, Hope for America

"This much-needed book will foster a deeper appreciation for the Holy Scripture by Christians, when compared to the teachings of the Qur'an. I recommend this excellent work to God's people everywhere and will use it myself in my own study with Muslim friends." — D. Eddie Bhawanie, professor of New Testament studies, American University of Biblical Studies

"Addressing the volatile issue of Islam and Christianity, this practical masterpiece, written from a Reformed perspective, should be read by both pastors and their parishioners." —Darlene M. Quinn, manager of telephone services for publisher, Nashville

THE
TRUTH
ABOUT
ISLAM

THE
TRUTH
ABOUT
ISLAM

THE NOBLE QUR'AN'S TEACHINGS
IN LIGHT OF THE HOLY BIBLE

ANEES ZAKA & DIANE COLEMAN

P&R
PUBLISHING
P.O. BOX 817 • PHILLIPSBURG • NEW JERSEY 08865-0817

Unless otherwise indicated, all Scripture quotations are from the HOLY BIBLE, NEW INTERNATIONAL VERSION®. NIV®. Copyright © 1973, 1978, 1984 by International Bible Society. Used by permission of Zondervan Publishing House. All rights reserved.

Scripture quotations marked NKJV are from The Holy Bible, New King James Version. Copyright © 1979, 1980, 1982, Thomas Nelson, Inc.

Page design and typesetting by Lakeside Design Plus

Printed in the United States of America

Library of Congress Cataloging-in-Publication Data

Zaka, Anees, 1942–
    The truth about Islam : the noble Qur'an's teachings in light of the Holy Bible / Anees Zaka and Diane Coleman.
        p. cm.
    Includes bibliographical references and index.
    Contents: "Truth" in Qur'anic Islam and Biblical thought—The truth about Muhammad—Jesus Christ in Qur'anic and Biblical thought—The Noble Qur'an and the Holy Bible—The godhead in Qur'anic and Biblical thought—Qur'anic and Biblical living: law and grace—Communicating the gospel of grace to Muslims.
    ISBN 0-87552-621-7 (paper)
    1. Islam—Controversial literature. 2. Islam—Relations—Christianity. 3. Christianity and other religions—Islam. I. Coleman, Diane, 1955– II. Title.

BT1170.Z34 2004
261.2'6—dc22

                                                    2004044511

To

Our Lord and Savior Jesus Christ,
who alone is the Way, the Truth, and the Life

The families God has given us,
natural and "adopted through Christ"

Sincere Truth-seekers everywhere

True statesmen of our country

Every faithful Bible preacher and teacher in our land,
especially those in the Presbyterian Church in America

The loving memory of the late Dr. James M. Boice,
who preached, taught, and lived
the truth of the gospel

CONTENTS

LIST OF TABLES

FOREWORD

Wwhen Pilate asked Jesus, "What is truth?" (John 18:38), he posed the supreme question of all of life. But he also posed the most ironic question of all of history. Standing on trial before him was the one who claimed to be "the truth" (John 14:6) and the one who "came into the world to testify to the truth" (John 18:37). In fact, Jesus declared, "Everyone on the side of truth listens to me" (John 18:37).

Obviously, the quest for Truth and the confrontation over truth claims did not begin in Pilate's tribunal. Nor did they end there. From Adam's encounter with two different assertions of truth in Eden (Gen. 2:16–17; 3:1–5), to Copernicus's *De Revolutionibus* in the Papal Court, to Luther at the Diet of Worms, to the Founding Fathers of Independence Hall, to Hitler's *Mein Kampf* and the Holocaust, to the fire and debris of the World Trade Center on 9/11, the cataclysmic implications of the disagreement over Truth have defined the course of human destiny.

What makes Dr. Anees Zaka's and Mrs. Diane Coleman's *The Truth about Islam* such an important and compelling work as well as necessary reading for our moment in history is that it insists that Truth exists, and that the claims for Truth made by both Christianity and Islam must be taken seriously—not only by their own religious adherents, but by all who share life in a pluralistic culture.

Pushing aside certain cultural leaders' "politically correct" platitudes that encourage us to believe that truth is only personal and therefore entirely relative, our authors declare that the teachings of Islam and Christianity are clear and distinct, and that those doctrines result in powerfully different views of reality, behavior, and culture.

Whether one approaches this book holding to the authors' sincere and deeply held conviction that Christianity is true, or to the Noble Qur'an's opposite view of Truth, or even to agnosticism's or secular liberalism's total uncertainty regarding Truth characteristics, this study makes one thing clear: Islam and Christianity cannot both be true.

Zaka and Coleman take us to the original sources—the Holy Scriptures and the Noble Qur'an—to compare each faith's holy text point for point. They do so with conviction, but also with careful scholarship and sincere respect. Their task is apologetic in nature, but their defense of Truth does not lose sight of the ideal of "speaking the truth in love."

The Truth about Islam, then, is a timely and practical book. The reader interested in the defense of the Christian faith or in missionary and evangelistic outreach will find help for the task. But a sincere Muslim will also be aided by reading this work in learning how a Christian student of Islam views that faith. An unbeliever in Christianity or Islam will be assisted as well in understanding how these two competing faiths contrast based on their official sources.

On a personal note, as one who is deeply concerned both as a pastor and as director of an educational organization committed to reinstilling in our culture the Judeo-Christian values of America's Founding Fathers, I am grateful that the fruits of our authors' research are capsulized in such thorough and helpful summaries and charts.

And finally, it is certainly helpful for me as a defender and promoter of religious liberty to know that the Noble Qur'an says in Sura 9:29,

> Fight those who do not believe in Allah nor the Last Day, nor hold that forbidden which has been forbidden by Allah and His Messenger, nor acknowledge the Religion of Truth, (even if they are) of the People of the Book [i.e., Christianity], until they pay the Jizya [tax] with willing submission, and feel themselves subdued.

It is also important for me to know that the Holy Scriptures say, "Do to others what you would have them do to you" (Matt. 7:12) and "Love your enemies and pray for those who persecute you" (Matt. 5:44).

Peter A. Lillback, Ph.D., Senior Pastor
Proclamation Presbyterian Church
Bryn Mawr, Pennsylvania

PREFACE

This book is unique in several ways. First, its two authors have contrasting backgrounds: one Western, one Eastern. Both are American citizens and united in fellowship with Christ Jesus through his saving grace. Christ is Lord over all, and in him there is no East or West. Nonetheless, with their diverse backgrounds the authors are able to view issues of faith from differing cultural vantage points. Second, hundreds of Christians bathed the authors in prayer and fasting throughout the book's development. Third, the Qur'anic and biblical texts have been assembled in tables, sometimes placed side by side to facilitate study. Sincere Truth-seekers will be helped by this clear presentation of the actual words of both documents.

We have focused on telling the Truth in love. "Truth matters supremely," writes Os Guinness, "because in the end, without truth there is no freedom. Truth, in fact, is not only essential to freedom; it *is* freedom, and the only way to a free life lies in becoming a person of truth and learning to live in truth. Living in truth is the secret of living free."[1]

But Truth, especially about ourselves, is seldom sweet. In fact, it is almost invariably bitter and is, for many ears, hard to hear. A great measure of Truth is included in this book, including the ultimate conviction that *Jesus is the Way, the Truth, and the Life,* and that *no one comes to the Father except through him.*

This may be an offensive position to some. Although it is not our intent to alienate anyone or be viewed as adversarial, this Truth was given to us by the Creator of the universe, and we, as biblical Christians, are commissioned and committed to deliver this good news to all. We pray for special blessing upon those who read it with earnest minds and open hearts. The authors also wholeheartedly welcome, through the publisher, readers' sincere inquiries.

It is with grateful thanksgiving and devoted worship that we offer this humble work to Christ alone. We pray that it will be pleasing in his sight, and we give him all the glory, the honor, and the majesty in his church worldwide, now and forevermore. Amen.

Anees Zaka

ACKNOWLEDGMENTS

The authors would like to thank their beloved spouses: Fareda, wife of Anees, and Jeffrey, husband of Diane. Jeff wisely counseled the writers in the development of their working relationship and exhibited unbounded patience. Fareda demonstrated generous and loving hospitality, sharing her delicious homemade baklava and her cozy slippers.

Additional thanks go to faithful daughters Allison and Juliana, who endured long days as their mother sat at the computer. The grace of God rested upon them continually.

Special gratitude is due to Robert Delancy of CLC and to Alfred A. Z. Siha for their skillful and necessary editorial assistance in preparing the final manuscript.

Humble thanksgiving goes to Proclamation Presbyterian Church (PCA) in Bryn Mawr, Pennsylvania, for its generous year-end gift, which helped meet the financial expense of preparing the manuscript.

Finally, heartfelt thanks go to all the committed biblical Christians around the world who faithfully lifted the authors in prayer during the writing. Their petitions for help and guidance were graciously answered by our great God and King. It is a continual joy and delight to serve him with devoted heart, soul, mind, and strength.

"A Prayer for the Muslim World"

Almighty God,
our heavenly Father,
who hast made of one blood
all nations
and hast promised
that many shall come
from the East
and sit down with Abraham
in thy kingdom:
We pray for
thy prodigal children
in Muslim lands
who are still afar off,
that they may be brought nigh
by the blood of Christ.
Look upon them in pity,
because they are ignorant
of thy truth . . .

INTRODUCTION

T*he Truth about Islam*—a bold title. But Truth is a bold thing. It is not driven by public-opinion polls. Nor can it be manufactured by hyped-up emotion or straitjacketed by flawed human reason. Truth stands firm against a kaleidoscope of cultural forces and is not judged by any human court. It is eternal and infinite. Truth is Divine.

People claim to love and seek Truth. Throughout the ages men have praised its pursuit in poetry and prose, song and sophistry. It appears elusive and unattainable. Truth is so encompassing, so brilliantly complex, so elegant in its harmony and coherence that it surpasses the full comprehension of any mortal. Truth is above and beyond finding out by man-made efforts, residing in the realm of religion, to be apprehended only by faith.

Qur'anic Islam claims to be the faith of Truth, capitalizing the word *Truth* to underscore belief in its divine origin. Islam presents itself as a kissing cousin of Judaism and Christianity and the champion of uncompromising monotheism, with Allah as its sole object of worship. Muhammad is regarded as the final prophet of Allah. The Noble Qur'an, which is the preferred title of Islam's sacred book, is revered as Allah's final word.

1

Biblical Christianity also lays claim to being the faith of Truth, capitalizing the word *Truth* to honor it as the primary characteristic of and alternative name for the biblical Triune God, Yahweh. *Triune* means "three in one." God the Father reveals himself to humanity in his Son, Jesus Christ, and manifests himself through the power of the Holy Spirit. Three Persons—Father, Son, and Holy Spirit—make up the Godhead. Given the title "Messiah" or "Christ," Jesus is proclaimed as the only Savior of humankind, fulfilling biblical Old Testament prophecy. The books of the biblical New Testament bear witness to his life and mission. Jesus Christ, according to biblical Christians, is Yahweh's complete and final Word to man and the fullest revelation of Divine Truth.

We have here two very different belief systems. But recently many Muslim and Christian religious leaders have been publicly proclaiming that Islam and Christianity are not so very different. In the book *Islam: A Global Civilization*, prepared and published by the Islamic Affairs Department of the Embassy of Saudi Arabia in Washington, D.C., we read:

One should in fact properly speak of the Judeo-Christian-Islamic tradition, for Islam shares with the other Abrahamic religions their sacred history, the basic ethical teachings contained in the Ten Commandments and above all, belief in the One God. And it renews and repeats the true beliefs of Jews and Christians whose scriptures are mentioned as divinely revealed books in Islam's own sacred book, the Qur'an.[1]

This presentation of Islam by Saudi Arabian nationals clearly claims continuity with Judeo-Christian thought. It echoes the frequently heard "politically correct" view that truth can take many forms and present itself in many ways, with Judaism, Christianity, and Islam being "separate paths on the same mountain to the same God." This approach, while acknowledging differences between the belief systems, essentially states that those differences don't ultimately matter. In the effort to find common ground, this perspective blurs the defining edges of all three faiths.

But the edges of Islam have come into sharper focus since September 11, 2001. The intense spotlights that illuminated the burial mounds of debris from the destruction of the World Trade Center have now been trained on Islam. Just as the tower debris was minutely sifted to detect any precious remains of humanity, so too must Islam be sifted to find out what it holds in relation to the Truth.

Religious discussion today follows the drumbeat of secular pundits and media analysts—not the best-qualified participants in this debate. Spiritual truths cannot be reduced to sound bites or painted in broad conceptual strokes. Muslims and Christians have a plethora of misperceptions about one another. Honest and forthright dialogue between believers of both faiths cannot take place when truths about either religion are glossed over, taken out of context, or embellished with falsehood.

Since the attack on the United States—which was, by any sane and moral standard, an evil and appalling deed—many books have been written about Islam: some by Muslims, some by Christians, some by humanists or secularists. These books vary widely in value, some of them suffering from inadvertent inaccuracy, careless attack of one religion or the other (or both), or dangerous compromise of historic biblical Christian faith.

This book is written on the presuppositional conviction that the One True God reveals himself and his Truth in the Holy Bible. We are certain, based on many convincing proofs, that the text of the Holy Bible has not been corrupted but is a document we can trust to define biblical Christianity. We therefore rely on it as our standard for evaluating all other philosophical or religious positions so that every thought is made obedient to the Lord Jesus Christ (2 Cor. 10:5), who is Lord of all.

Greg L. Bahnsen, in his book *Always Ready*, articulates this position clearly:

> The word of the Lord is self-attestingly true and authoritative. It is the criterion we must use in judging all other words. Thus, God's word is unassailable. It must be the rock-bottom foundation of our thinking and living (Matt. 7:24–25). It is our presuppositional starting-point. All our reasoning must be subordinated to God's word, for no man is in a position to reply against it (Rom. 9:20) and any who contend with God will end up having to answer (Job 40:1–5). It must not be the changing opinions of men but the self-attesting, authoritative, ultimately veracious word from God that has the preeminence in our thoughts, for "canst thou thunder with a voice like Him?" (Job 40:9).[2]

We invite serious and reasonable people of all faiths, particularly those of Islam and Christianity, to read this book with the above understanding in order to derive benefit from it.

4

As our primary source document for Islam, we will quote from the Noble Qur'an as interpreted into English by Abdullah Yusuf Ali (2001 edition). Various Hadiths and Sunnahs (sayings and practices of Muhammad) are cited, since these expand on Qur'anic themes and are used by Islamic religious leaders to define doctrine and develop religious practices. Finally, we occasionally refer to noted Islamic commentators, such as Al-Ghazali, who have been strongly influential in the theological development of Islam.

For biblical references we quote primarily the New International Version of the Holy Bible (1984 edition, International Bible Society). Additionally, major scholars and theologians within the Reformed and Calvinistic tradition of biblical Christianity, past and present, are cited for authoritative exegesis and in-depth analysis.

Many of these excerpts are presented in tables for ease of review. Readers are strongly encouraged to obtain copies of both the Noble Qur'an and the Holy Bible and to read the cited passages completely and within context. Only honest examination of the original doctrinal and historical source texts of each religion and the behaviors taught to believers based on those sources will help us to understand each faith—particularly the truth about Islam.

By presenting information in this manner, we are not seeking to conduct a comparative study between the two faiths. Biblical Christianity and Qur'anic Islam are not equal in terms of doctrine or behavior and are therefore not in that sense comparable. The former represents Divine Truth, the whole Truth, and nothing but the Truth. The latter is a reflection of a particular personality, time, and place, and, as we will see, seriously deviates from the central message of the Old and New Testaments to which it links itself. Because of this linkage, it is altogether fitting that we should evaluate Islam in the light of the Holy Bible, which Islam itself acknowledges as revelatory in some Qur'anic passages.

When Qur'anic passages seem to reflect some measure of consistency with biblical thought, this is not to be taken as a verification that the Noble Qur'an in its entirety is Divine Truth. There may be points of apparent intersection within the faith traditions, but these are less congruous than they may at first appear.

At the same time, we want to make it clear that sincere and honest questioning of Islamic doctrine and practice does not constitute, and is not intended as, aggression against adherents of that faith. The dialectic approach we take is an effective means of accurately communicating ideas. We intend no disrespect to the Muslim community by our use of probing analytical questions or philosophical rhetoric. This is one of the ways in which Truth is discerned by rational and relational beings.

The Noble Qur'an asserts in Sura 5:82:

> And nearest among them in love to the Believers [Muslims] will you find those who say, "We are Christians": because amongst these are men devoted to learning and men who have renounced the world, and they are not arrogant.

First Peter 3:15 says:

> But in your hearts set apart Christ as Lord. Always be prepared to give an answer to everyone who asks you to give the reason for the hope that you have. But do this with gentleness and respect, keeping a clear

conscience, so that those who speak maliciously against your good behavior in Christ may be ashamed of their slander.

We commit this work to the ministry of the Holy Spirit, who alone is able to use it as a means of grace for those whom he chooses to call to himself. May our great and loving Heavenly Father receive all the glory for our humble effort.

1

"TRUTH" IN QUR'ANIC ISLAM AND BIBLICAL CHRISTIANITY

What is the truth about "Truth"? This is not an exercise in semantic gymnastics. Truth is not a hopelessly abstract idea or a nebulous gut feeling; it is a divine reality. It has characteristics—truths—about it that make it identifiable and knowable. Several of these are familiar to us all.

Judicial proceedings throughout the free world and in Muslim nations require that witnesses promise to tell "the truth, the whole truth, and nothing but the truth." Why are these parameters so clearly and separately defined? The reason is that it is very possible to tell partial truth by withholding or distorting certain facts. It is also possible to add to the truth by bringing in extraneous information, thereby putting a misleading spin on the facts. The oath is designed to prevent these kinds of errors.

Divine Truth, proceeding from the mind of God, more than satisfies the characteristics of judicial truth-telling. It is "true Truth" (in the words of Christian philosopher and theologian Francis Schaeffer)—consistent, faithful, dependable, and pure, not contaminated with any error. It is the whole Truth, not partial or incomplete, not requiring anything apart from itself to confirm or substantiate it. And it is nothing but the Truth, without superfluous, misleading, or distracting information.

Divine Truth must be nothing short of perfect. And this is, indeed, what biblical Christianity proclaims.

RELATIVISM AS TRUTH

Where do people go to find Truth these days? Confronted with the bewildering number of belief systems claiming to have the Truth, many people have thrown up their hands and chosen the easy path, which is the philosophy of relativism. Its premise is simple: "Truth is relative. What's true for me may or may not be true for you. It may be true for me in one instance and not in another. I have my own idea of what is true, and who's to say it's not?"

In his book *Renewing the Soul of America,* Charles Crismier counters, "Truth must be what it is and ought to be, not what I want it to be."[1] Relativism is a capricious approach to Truth. Its most obvious flaw is that it is internally inconsistent. It commits what it condemns by asserting one absolute truth: that there is not and never has been an authority on earth possessing objective Truth applicable to all people at all times. By stating this, relativism itself becomes dogmatic. As Ibn Warraq explains, "There is something inherently illogical in relativism. Relativism can't be stated, because the proposition that expounds relativism cannot itself be relative."[2]

10

So we must discard relativism as a means for arriving at Divine Truth.

SCIENCE AS TRUTH

Others have embraced science as the foundation of knowledge. In that view Truth must be observable, reproducible, and measurable. At best, however, scientific laws derived by human experience give us *truths*, or portions of the Truth, but not the whole Truth and nothing but the Truth. Scientific truths are never complete, nor are they fully dependable. New discoveries often challenge previous "laws." Experimental results sometimes yield conflicting information and require additional protocols to confirm theories, which may later give way to new findings. Science broadens our working knowledge of our physical environment but can never be an efficient tool for understanding spiritual realities such as love, compassion, goodness, and honor.

So, although science can be of service in describing some truths within a larger framework, it too must be discarded as an autonomous criterion or a means of arriving at complete Divine Truth.

TRUTH MUST MAKE ITSELF KNOWN

If we were to proceed through all the disciplines and philosophies of man, we would find none of them, alone or together, sufficient to discover the truth about Divine Truth. Divine Truth, if it is to be known, must somehow take the initiative and reveal itself to us.

11

THE MORAL LAW

All people are religious. We all believe in something. Some of our beliefs are startlingly consistent across time and space. Warraq, quoting Isaiah Berlin, comments: "No culture that we know lacks the notions of good and bad; true and false. Courage, for example, has, so far as we can tell, been admired in every society known to us. There are universal values. This is an empirical fact about mankind."[3] It is *empirical* because it is something that can be verified by observation or experience, namely our own human behavior.

This consistency among cross-cultural values is referred to as the "moral law," implanted within human conscience as a means of internal control. Oxford scholar C. S. Lewis, in his masterly work *Mere Christianity*, explains, "We conclude that the Being behind the universe is intensely interested in right conduct—in fair play, unselfishness, courage, good faith, honesty, and truthfulness."[4] All the common cultural virtues have Truth at their core—and as their source.

Why do we call the moral law a "law"? It is not like a scientific law, which is inferred from observable behaviors or outcomes. For instance, we know that gravity exists because objects always fall downward. Yet we do not receive our notions of moral law based on what we observe ourselves doing, but from an innate sense that we *should* do right, a sense properly enlightened by scriptural revelation of what "right" is.

In many cases, our sense of responsibility is in antithesis to the acts we actually commit. Human beings frequently behave in ways that are unfair, selfish, cowardly, faithless, dishonest, and deceitful. Although we attempt to justify and often condone such wrong behaviors in creative ways, we can never completely erase some sense of morality. Though a few may tragically twist and distort their sense of duty to the point of flying fully loaded planes into civilian buildings, there remains a prevailing sense among us that this is appallingly evil. Even when we do not agree on what is right and what is wrong, we all believe—religiously—that some things are right and others are wrong. And amazingly often, despite religious and cultural differences, we do express a shared innate moral sense of where to draw the line.

Lewis concludes that the implantation of this moral law is the way in which the God of the universe makes himself known to us. The Divine Being takes the initiative and reveals himself to us. Having a conscience is a gift from God to assist us in discerning Truth. Biblical Christians often call this gift God's "common grace."

The natural human response to this phenomenon throughout history in every culture—so natural that it must be suppressed to avoid it—has been to ask, Who is behind this moral law? What is his Truth? Who or what can we trust to teach us about his Truth? When we know this Truth, *how should we respond?*

TRUTH IN QUR'ANIC ISLAM

In Islam, the divine source of Truth is Allah, whose name is most often defined by Muslims as "the God." In Islamic thought, the main focus of the concept of Truth is not on knowing Allah in a relational way, but on affirming the revelation that Muhammad received (the Noble Qur'an) and defending him as the final prophet of Allah.

The holy texts of Islam—the Noble Qur'an, the Hadiths (sayings of the prophet Muhammad), and the Sunnah (prac-

13

tices of Muhammad)—represent the fullest expression of Truth to Muslims. The law of Allah (shari'ah) in these texts is Allah's will for man. The response of the Muslim is to submit to this law, with its attendant rites and rituals, in the hope of pleasing Allah and attaining personal reward, both here and in the hereafter.

Failure to submit results in eternal damnation: "If anyone contends with the Messenger even after guidance has been plainly conveyed to him, and follows a path other than that becoming to men of Faith, We shall leave him in the path he has chosen, and land him in Hell,—what an evil refuge!" (Sura 4:115).

TRUTH IN BIBLICAL CHRISTIANITY

The Zondervan Exhaustive Concordance for the New International Version of the Holy Bible lists well over two hundred passages containing the word *truth*. In the book of Matthew alone, Jesus says, "I tell you the truth" more than 30 times to call attention to a main point of teaching. Clearly, Truth is a very important concept within biblical thought.

Christians believe that Truth is fully revealed in the life, death, and resurrection of a divine Person, Jesus Christ. The Triune God, Yahweh (whose name means, "I was, I am, I will be"), chose to make himself known to his people through his Son. Jesus boldly proclaims in John 14:6, "I am the way and the truth and the life. No one comes to the Father except through me." This is as startling a statement today as it was for first-century listeners! In essence, Jesus is saying: "I am (Yahweh) Truth (the Way and Life)."

Biblical Christianity maintains that Jesus, the perfect representation of Yahweh, is Truth personified (Eph. 4:21). The main focus of Divine Truth is to bring repentant people into a personal relationship with Jesus Christ, thereby redeeming them from the sentence of eternal separation from Yahweh. This is salvation for the Christian.

REDEMPTION AND SALVATION

The twin ideas of "redemption" and "salvation" are ancient ones. Used in the books of Exodus and Psalms to describe Yahweh's action in delivering the Israelites from slavery in Egypt, *redemption* is the release of something or someone from bondage or possession through the payment of a redemption price. This deliverance does not come cheaply. It is, in fact, a costly thing and often demands a high payment, which can only be described as sacrificial.

Christian theology states that man, because of his sin nature inherited from Adam and Eve, cannot come into the presence of the perfect and holy God, Yahweh, and cannot have full communion with him. Man has fallen and is under the sentence of death and separation from Yahweh, both on earth and in eternity. But Yahweh desires to have fellowship with each man and woman, for he has created them in his own image as relational beings.

By God's own justice, the price to be paid in order to release someone from this bondage to sin and death is the submission of a perfect will to him, resulting in total and complete righteousness, culminating in the final act of the shedding of blood through the physical death of the earthly body as a perfect sacrifice. This is indeed a costly redemption!

No mere man can accomplish this. No mere mortal can offer perfect submission of his will to Yahweh, nor will the death of his imperfect body yield the perfect blood sacrifice

15

necessary to redeem himself or anyone else. No mere man in history is able to become fully righteous and follow the divinely implanted moral law perfectly by his own effort, no matter how sincere he may be or how hard he tries. Romans 3:23 states that "all have sinned and fall short of the glory of God."

Man is corrupted by sin and inclined to rebellion. We need only look at ourselves to see that this is true. We are traitors to the Truth and habitual violators of the moral law. This understanding leads biblical Christians to brokenhearted repentance and the realization that our only hope for deliverance is in our dependence on a gracious Savior. This was the response of the people in Acts 2:38: "Peter replied, 'Repent and be baptized, every one of you, in the name of Jesus Christ so that your sins may be forgiven.' "

Thus, we arrive at the central concept of salvation. Christians believe that God's incredibly loving plan was to redeem, or buy back, his people by paying their debt for them, graciously offering himself in the perfect Person of Jesus Christ, his Son. Ephesians 1:7–8 states: "In him [Jesus] we have redemption through his blood, the forgiveness of sins, in accordance with the riches of God's grace that he lavished on us with all wisdom and understanding." This is what Christians hold to be the truth about the Truth of Holy Scripture, from Genesis to Revelation.

THE NEED FOR REDEMPTION

Truth in biblical thought is always redemptive. Truth in Islamic thought is never redemptive. In biblical Christianity, God compassionately brings his people to himself. In

16

Islam, Allah is considered "wholly other" and entirely separated from his people.[5] Allah redeems no one.

Although Islam claims descent from Judeo-Christian thought and purports to honor the "previous Scripture," which is the Holy Bible, salvation through redemption by another is a completely alien idea to Muslims. The acknowledgment of sinners' basic need for salvation is entirely absent from Islamic thought. The message of Islam "concerns men and women as they were created by God—not as fallen beings."[6] Muslims do not recognize the inherent sin nature of man. Violation of the law of Allah is simply due to human forgetfulness, not because of any internal corruption. Repetitive prayer and Qur'anic recitation are established to assist man's poor memory. "[Faith] means to remember God [Allah] at all times, and marks the highest level of being a Muslim."[7]

MORAL LAW REPLACED

The moral law, implanted within man by Yahweh's common grace, is effectively replaced in Islam with prescribed public behaviors of devotion. Strong community pressure is applied to ensure observance. These behaviors are the primary means for overcoming human forgetfulness and achieving a higher level of submission to Allah.

Publicly enforced devotional behaviors have a tendency to impart a sense of false security to those who engage in them. Some Christian groups adhere to similar kinds of practices. But such behaviors among Christians are generally extrabiblical rituals, established and maintained by human tradition and not sanctioned by Scripture. In Islam, however, public devotional behaviors are derived from and intrinsic to the Qur'anic message.

17

All deep religious thinkers must agree that ritualistic behaviors are insufficient to meet the spiritual demands of a pure and holy Deity or the spiritual needs of man. Disciplines such as prayer, fasting, and tithing are important in the exercise of biblical Christian faith, but they are only carnal and meaningless motions if not motivated by a loving relationship with the biblical Triune God. They can never fully satisfy man's fundamental need, which is salvation from the bondage of sin, divine forgiveness, and true communion with the Triune God, both in time and in eternity.

BELIEF IN ACTION

This relationship with the Heavenly Father through Jesus Christ has a tremendous impact on the way in which biblical Christians live their lives. Salvation's certainty for the believer has a liberating effect, freeing him from the bondage of habitual sin. Human beings can never be perfect in their earthly existence, but those who are called to be God's adopted children through Christ are no longer compelled to blindly follow their own corrupted wills.

The Holy Spirit, the third Person of the Triune God, enters into the "temple" of the Christian, as we read in 1 Corinthians 6:19: "Do you not know that your body is a temple of the Holy Spirit, who is in you, whom you have received from God?" The Spirit enables, empowers, and teaches him to "conduct [himself] in a manner worthy of the gospel of Christ" (Phil. 1:27).

The Holy Spirit is the sanctifier of the Christian conscience and inscribes the moral law on the hearts of believers, who are to conduct themselves accordingly.

18

This is biblical belief in action. The apostle Paul continually asks the question "Do you not know . . . ?" and appeals to the knowledge of his readers in his letter to the Romans (6:3, 16; 7:1) and his first letter to the Corinthians (3:16; 5:6; 6:2–3, 9, 15–16, 19; 9:13, 24). He emphasizes that knowing the Truth in Christ and being guided by the active grace of the Holy Spirit will ultimately be manifested in right *living*, which is a greater accomplishment than right *doing*. Any Christian who claims to know the Truth of Christianity and does not live it through the strength of the Holy Spirit is a hypocrite with a false claim to virtue.

ISLAMIC FAITH AND VIRTUE

Islamic faith means "having faith in God [Allah], His angels, His books, His messengers, the Day of Judgment and God's determination of human destiny."[8] Islamic virtue "means to worship God as if one sees Him, knowing that even if one does not see Him, He sees us."[9]

Islamic faith is primarily a verbal agreement with a set of doctrinal statements and visible participation in acts affirming this agreement to others and to Allah. Admits Farid Esack, internationally known South African Muslim scholar and currently the Brueggemann Chair in Interreligious Studies at Xavier University in Cincinnati, Ohio, "One can be totally committed to Islam and yet not have it touch one's inner being."[10] He goes on to confess that "our lives as Muslims are largely devoid of an ongoing and living connection with Allah."[11] This deeply human cry for a relationship with the Divine causes the Christian's heart to break with compassion.

19

THE JOURNEY OF FAITH

Faith is rightly compared to a journey. When one goes on a journey, the course must be charted and maintained without deviation. Small variations along the way must constantly be detected and corrected. A single degree of change, followed without correction, will bring one to a final destination many miles from the original goal.

TABLE 1 According to the Noble Qur'an, Islam is . . .

Characteristic	Sura
the religion accepted by Allah	3:19–20, 84; 110:2
a better religion, requiring man to submit to Allah	2:112; 4:125
bowing to Allah, no one else	6:14, 71, 125; 39:12, 22, 54
believing in Allah and his messenger (Muhammad)	9:74
Muhammad's way	109:6
worshiping Allah	10:104–5
a revelation sent down with the knowledge of Allah	11:14
Allah's favor on men that bow to his will	16:81
Allah's favor upon you	49:17
submitting your will to Allah, who is one	22:34; 27:31, 42, 81
coming to Allah in full submission	49:14
bowing before the lord of the worlds	40:66
calling men to Allah to bow	41:33
believing in the signs of Muhammad and bowing your will to him	43:69
a chosen religion by Allah for you	5:3; 24:55
holding fast to Allah	22:78
the religion of the prophets	42:13
the religion of Truth	9:29, 33; 48:28; 61:9
the most trustworthy religion	2:256; 31:22
the right religion	12:40; 30:30; 45:18
the word of Allah	9:6
desired by unbelievers	15:2
an invitation to all	61:7

This is also true for religion. No matter how valid the starting point may be, religious belief will arrive at the wrong destination if it stays on a steady course that deviates a fraction from the original. This is the great deceit of false religion. It often contains *just enough* truth to appear valid. The course readings *seem* true and consistent. But the follower of such a faith is astonished at the end of life's journey to find himself in a very different place from his expected destination. The right course of faith must originate in pure Truth and continue in the whole Truth and nothing but the Truth. Only then will it lead to the glorious destination of eternal fellowship with God.

So let's examine the courses of Islam and Christianity, defined by their sacred documents. Table 1, taken from the Church Without Walls (CWW) Educational Materials, summarizes the Qur'anic passages that define Islam. As you examine Qur'anic teachings about Islam, the following conclusions become apparent:

- Qur'anic Islam is submission to Allah, as a slave submits to his master. It is not a relationship between man and God.
- Qur'anic Islam is to bow before Allah out of fear and not out of love. It is not a fellowship between man and his Creator.
- Qur'anic Islam is a religion of good works, generally defined as physical acts of worship and public devotion. It is not a union between man and God.
- Qur'anic Islam is what you do for Allah, not what Allah does for you. It is not a personal experience of man with God.

21

HISTORICAL BIBLICAL VIEW OF ISLAM

Qur'anic Islam was well known to the Reformers and fathers of the faith. Martin Luther (1463–1546) regarded it as God's judgment upon Roman corruption, a rod of correction for our sin, and the religion of the "natural man." He called upon the church to pray, repent, and go back to the Word as a means of stopping Islam's influence in the world.

John Calvin (1509–64) stated that Islam was not to be compared to the "True religion," according to the Word of God. He compared it to the teachings of the Pharisees or the papal doctrines appended to the gospels. Calvin noted the distorted biblical stories and rabbinical traditions found in the Noble Qur'an and highlighted its teaching as a departure from the pure and simple Word of God.

HADITHIC DEFINITIONS OF ISLAM

The sayings of Muhammad found in these Hadiths, translated by Thomas Cleary in his book *The Wisdom of the Prophet,* further elucidate the definition of Islam:

> One day the Prophet was sitting with some people when the archangel Gabriel came to him and said, "What is faith?"
>
> The Prophet replied, "Faith is to believe in God, in God's angels, and in meeting God; and in the messengers of God; and in the resurrection."
>
> Gabriel said, "What is submission?"
>
> The Prophet replied, "Submission is to serve God and not attribute any partners to God, and to pray

22

regularly, and to pay the prescribed welfare tax, and to fast during the month of Ramadan."

Gabriel said, "What is goodness?"

The Prophet replied, "To worship God as if you actually see God; for if you do not see God, God certainly sees you."[12]

Sufyan Bin Abdullah related, "I said to the Messenger of God, 'Tell me a statement on Islam such that I need ask no one else but you about it.' He told me, "Say, 'I believe in God,' and be upright."[13]

The Prophet said, "Religion is goodwill."

He was asked, "Toward whom?"

He said, "Toward God, and toward the Book of God, and toward the Messenger of God, and toward the imams of the Muslims, and toward their communities."[14]

These Hadiths speak for themselves.

What does the Holy Bible tell us about Christianity? The Scriptures in table 2 make the following conclusions clear:

- Biblical Christianity is a relationship between man and Jesus Christ, who is the only Savior of his people.
- Biblical Christianity is a restored fellowship and reconciliation between man and his Creator, through the intercession of Jesus Christ.
- Biblical Christianity is a union of man and God, in the Person of Jesus Christ, and in the heart of the Christian believer through the Holy Spirit.

23

TABLE 2 According to the Bible, Christianity means or is . . .

Characteristic	Reference
to live is Christ	Phil. 1:21
the power of God for the salvation of everyone who believes	Rom. 1:16
a righteousness that is by faith from first to last	Rom. 1:17
circumcision of the heart by the Spirit	Rom. 2:29
the message of the cross	1 Cor. 1:18
a new covenant—not of the letter but of the Spirit	2 Cor. 3:6
being transformed into Christ's likeness	2 Cor. 3:18
God was reconciling the world to himself in Christ	2 Cor. 5:19
revelation from Jesus Christ	Gal. 1:12
faith expressing itself through love	Gal. 5:6
to be adopted as his sons through Jesus Christ	Eph. 1:4
the gift of God—not by works, so that no one can boast	Eph. 2:9
built on the foundation of the apostles and prophets, with Christ Jesus himself as the chief cornerstone	Eph. 2:20
love that surpasses knowledge	Eph. 3:19
to put on the new self, created to be like God in true righteousness and holiness	Eph. 4:23–24
being like-minded . . . being one in spirit and purpose	Phil. 2:2
bearing fruit in every good work, growing in the knowledge of God, being strengthened with all power	Col. 1:10–11
the kingdom of the Son God loves	Col. 1:13–14
not trying to please men, but God	1 Thess. 2:4
putting on faith and love as a breastplate, and the hope of salvation as a helmet	1 Thess. 5:8–9
the appearing of our Savior, Christ Jesus, who has destroyed death and has brought life and immortality	2 Tim. 1:10
the washing of rebirth and renewal by the Holy Spirit, whom he poured out on us generously through Jesus Christ	Titus 3:5–6
to look after widows and orphans in their distress	James 1:27
obeying the truth . . . sincere love for your brothers	1 Peter 1:22
the victory that has overcome the world	1 John 5:4
understanding so that we may know him who is true	1 John 5:20
the right to the tree of life	Rev. 22:14
the free gift of the water of life	Rev. 22:17

24

- Biblical Christianity is a personal experience of man in relationship with God.
- Biblical Christianity is a life of dependence on and faith in Jesus Christ and his perfect life and sacrifice in our place. It is not a religion of good works that must be done to earn salvation or acceptance.
- Biblical Christianity is what God has done for man, not what man can do for God.
- Biblical Christianity is grateful servanthood toward others, in brotherly love.
- Biblical Christianity is an adoption as spiritual children of God, able to approach him as a loving Father, but in holy reverence, respect, and honor as Sovereign Lord.

BIBLICAL CHRISTIANITY IS CHRIST-CENTERED

Biblical Christianity is summarized using three phrases, according to CWW Educational Tract 1:

Faith in Christ
Fellowship with Christ
Following after Christ

The common denominator of these phrases is Christ. In him, Truth is personified. Those who are in Christ exhibit the characteristics shown in table 3, taken from the October 2002 Congregational Record and Bible Reading Notes of Immanuel Presbyterian Church in Norfolk, Virginia.

Faith does not come by rituals of modern religion, the often-flawed witness of believers, the ability to recite the creeds or doctrines of specific denominations, or the out-

TABLE 3   If you are in Christ Jesus by grace through faith, you . . .

Description	Reference
are justified and have peace with God	Rom. 5:1
have died with Christ and to the power of sin's rule	Rom. 6:1–6
are free from condemnation forever	Rom. 8:1
have Christ as your wisdom, righteousness, sanctification, and redemption	1 Cor. 1:30; 2 Cor. 5:21
have the mind of Christ	1 Cor. 2:16
are a temple of the Holy Spirit, bought with a price, not your own	1 Cor. 6:19–20
are established in Christ, sealed, and given the Spirit in your heart as a guarantee of your inheritance	2 Cor. 1:21; Eph. 1:13–14
are crucified with Christ and he lives in you	Gal. 2:20
are blessed with every spiritual blessing in Christ	Eph. 1:3
are chosen in Christ before the foundation of the world, that you should be holy and without blame before him in love	Eph. 1:4
are predestined to adoption as sons of God	Eph. 1:5; 1 John 3:1
are made alive together with Christ	Eph. 2:5
are made to sit in the heavenly places in Christ Jesus	Eph. 2:6
have access by one Spirit to the Father	Eph. 2:18
have boldness and access with confidence through faith in him	Eph. 3:12
are delivered from the power of darkness and conveyed into the kingdom of the Son of his love	Col. 1:13–14
have Christ in you	Col. 1:27
are a slave of righteousness and God	Rom. 6:18, 22
are an heir of God and joint heir with Christ	Rom. 8:17
are complete in Christ	Col. 2:10
are given a spirit of power and of love and of a sound mind	2 Tim. 1:7
are sanctified and one with the sanctifier, therefore Jesus calls you his brother	Heb. 2:11
are able to come boldly to the throne of grace to obtain mercy and find grace to help in time of need	Heb. 4:16
have been given exceedingly great and precious promises and become partakers of the divine nature	2 Peter 1:4
are the salt of the earth and the light of the world	Matt. 5:13–14
are Jesus' friend	John 15:15
are chosen by Jesus and appointed by him to bear lasting fruit	John 15:16

26

TABLE 3 (*continued*)

Description	Reference
are a member of the body of Christ	Eph. 5:30
are a new creation	2 Cor. 5:17
are a saint	Eph. 1:1
are holy and righteous	Eph. 4:24
are a life hidden with Christ in God	Col. 3:3
are the elect of God,, holy and beloved	Col. 3:12
are a chosen generation, a royal priesthood, a holy nation, his own special people, the people of God	1 Peter 2:9–10
have the ability to do all things through Christ who strengthens you	Phil 4:13
have all your needs supplied according to God's riches in glory by Christ Jesus	Phil 4:19
have the Lord as your strength and confidence	Ps. 27:1; Prov. 3:26
are being led by God to triumph in Christ	2 Cor. 2:14
are able to cast all your worries, fears, and anxieties on God	1 Peter 5:7
are never alone, for Christ is always with you	Matt. 28:20
have your sufficiency from God	2 Cor. 3:5
have God working in you to will and to do his good pleasure	Phil. 2:13
are able to live valiantly, for God will tread down your enemies	Ps. 60:12
will have fullness of joy and pleasures forevermore one day in God's very presence	Ps. 16:11
will have a far more exceeding and eternal weight of glory	2 Cor. 4:17
will have glory that shall be revealed in you	Rom. 8:18
will have no more tears, no more sorrow, no more pain	Rev. 21:4
are inseparable from the love of God in Christ	Rom. 8:35–39
have certain and unshakable promises causing you to be strong and fearless	Isa. 41:10
are one day to enter into the joy of your Lord	Matt. 25:23
are unable to be defeated	Rom. 8:31
are more than a conqueror through him who loved you	Rom. 8:37
have all things working for your good	Rom. 8:28
have your Heavenly Father pursuing you relentlessly with goodness and mercy all the days of your life	Ps. 23:6

ward observance of ceremonies or traditions associated with worship or lifestyle. The heart of biblical Christianity states that the only route to true paradise, which is never-ending companionship with the biblical Triune God, is complete faith and hope in Christ alone.

The fellowship between God and the believer starts while we are still in this life. The Christian faith is a very personal one and can flourish only if it is based on this ongoing relationship. Unlike the Qur'anic Allah, the biblical Yahweh wants to know his people and be known by them. This is a source of deep joy and abiding hope for the believer. As defined by theologian J. I. Packer, "Knowing God is a relationship calculated to thrill a man's heart."[15] Christ calls believers to follow him—which is no easy task! Christ must be the focus of all our endeavors. Christians are not called to lives of ease and comfort. We are called to lives of service and humility, following the example of Jesus Christ. This cannot be done without the help of the Holy Spirit.

Table 4 summarizes the basic characteristics of biblical Christianity and Qur'anic Islam.

TOUGH QUESTIONS

In expanding on the title *The Truth about Islam,* we must ask three revealing questions:

- Is Islam a divinely inspired faith, having all the characteristics of Divine Truth—or was it Muhammad's human attempt to unite the fragmented Arab people and convince them to abandon paganism?
- Is the Noble Qur'an a revelation of God, as it claims to be, like the Old and New Testaments that came

TABLE 4 Characteristics of Qur'anic Islam and biblical Christianity

Islam	Sura	Christianity	Reference
Human effort	3:132	Work of God	John 3:5
Tradition of men	Sunnah	God's grace	2 Peter 3:18
Earthly dress	33:59	Heavenly dress	Isa. 61:10
Regulated life	17:78	Radiant life	Matt. 5:16
Repressed conscience	58:2–3	Rebuilt character	Matt. 7:24
Fraternity of Ummah	2:143	Fellowship with Christ	Luke 24:32
Separation from Allah	42:49–50	Union with Yahweh	John 1:12
Direction	4:58–59	Discipleship	John 8:31–32
Submission	4:34–35	Service	1 Tim. 6:18
Limited sacrifice	47:36–37	Living sacrifice	Rom. 12:1
Walk alone	74:44–47	Walk with Christ	Col. 2:6
Physical warfare	9:73	Spiritual warfare	1 Tim. 6:12
Recitation and ritual	22:28–30	Running a race	Heb. 12:1
Cultural imperialism	3:110	Spiritual victory	1 John 5:4
Immortality with companions	37:45–49	Immortality with Christ	John 17:3

before it—or is it a document that Muhammad created from his many cross-cultural interactions during his early life as a merchant?

- Is Muhammad the "last of the prophets," as true prophets are defined according to biblical tradition— or was he a self-appointed messenger, exploiting the religious yearnings of a diverse populace for his own purposes?

The answers will be revealed to us in the light of Scripture and history.

29

"A Prayer for the Muslim World"
(continued)

. . . Take away pride of intellect
and blindness of heart,
and reveal to them
the surpassing beauty and power
of thy Son Jesus Christ.
Convince them
of their sin
in rejecting the atonement
of the only Savior.
Give moral courage
to those who love thee,
that they may boldly
confess thy name . . .

2

THE TRUTH ABOUT
MUHAMMAD

The Arabian peninsula in the seventh century A.D. was an active place. Crisscrossed with trade routes, it provided a convenient meeting place for people from East and West. Nations bought, sold, clashed, and formed alliances daily in this strategic and ancient land.

As goods changed hands, ideas changed minds. Christianity was spreading outward from Palestine, and groups of believers could be found throughout the Mediterranean basin. Jews dispersed across the area, and synagogues were established. Oriental mysticism traveled with the spices from the Far East. In short, the Arabian peninsula was a religious potpourri.

It may also be said that its people were a genetic potpourri:

Before Islam, there is not a single reference to a people known as the Arabs. None of the 21 references in the Qur'an to the Arabs talks of them as a people, a nation, or an ethnic group. There is not one reference to an Arab land, Arab rule, an Arab army, an Arab

31

man or woman. The Hadith does, however, use terms like Arab horse, Arab village and Arab book.[1]

The article goes on to describe the two forms of the word: *al-Arab,* meaning "desert dwellers"; and *Aaraabi,* used in conjunction with the Arabic language, tongue, book, or Qur'an. In the first sense, the Arab is described in terms that are decidedly unflattering, admonished as rebels, deceivers, backward, blasphemers, hypocrites, and enemies of Islam (Suras 9; 33:20; 48:11, 16–17; 49:14). In the second sense, it refers to one who "speaks with a straight, or clear, tongue."

The term can also be traced to roots in Aramaic, Hebrew, and Arabic. One thing is clear, "it did not refer to a homogeneous people who came from a certain ethnic background. Rather 'Arab' referred to 'intermixed' groups of people who lived in the deserts and spoke languages other than those spoken by the more established nations of the region."[2]

The Arab people are a diverse population, descended from a variety of racial and ethnic nomadic groups occupying the Arabian peninsula throughout its history. But they all had one thing in common—a yearning for the divine.

Muhammad grew up in an environment rich with religious fervor. His home was Mecca, the worship center of the Arab tribes. As a merchant, Muhammad depended for his livelihood on constant and successful interaction with the various trading groups entering the area. There is no question that he observed, discussed, and analyzed not only their wares, but their beliefs as well.

But the ideas and concepts given to him by those Christians whom he encountered did not often paint an accurate or complete picture of religious orthodoxy. Information was piecemeal and often based on hearsay—and heresy. Two extremes of theological thought arose and spread across Arabia and North Africa: Nestorianism, which denied the union of Christ's human and divine natures in his one Person, and Monophysitism, which combined the human and divine natures in one composite nature. Arabs who embraced Christianity often adopted one of these two views.

Few adherents of any faith had direct contact with knowledgeable spiritual leaders, still fewer with sacred books or writings. So what Muhammad eventually absorbed was a mishmash of fragmented biblical stories, miracle tales, and chronologically confused prophetic sayings—all regarded as authentic and equally truthful by the young merchant.

Prominent among the population were Jews, distinguished primarily from the Christians by their rejection of the messiahship of Jesus Christ. Consequently, they still looked eagerly toward the coming of their promised Savior, the "prophet like Moses."

Christians were anticipating the second coming of Jesus Christ. His first coming seven hundred years before had established a spiritual kingdom of God on earth, actively growing and being built up through the work of the Holy Spirit. His second coming, in his resurrected glory, would be to receive his spiritual children and establish his rule forever.

So the religious environment of Muhammad's time was highly charged with "messianic" expectation from both Jewish and Christian sectors, supported by the authoritative prophetic writings of the "Book," which included the Torah of the Jews and the Gospels of the Christians.

There was no doubt that initially Muhammad greatly admired both Jews and Christians. Equally important was his admiration for their prophets—those individuals chosen specifically by God to deliver his Word to his people. The fact that the Jews had once had a long line of divinely appointed individuals occupying the prophetic office, and that Christians enjoyed the full revelation of God in the "prophet" Jesus, was astonishing to Muhammad. Why had God not honored the Arabs in the same way?

And so it was that Muhammad began experiencing "revelations." These episodes were

> attended by a fit of unconsciousness, accompanied (or preceded) at times by the sound of bells in the ears or the belief that someone was present: by a sense of fright, such as to make the patient burst out into perspiration: by the turning of the head to one side: by foaming at the mouth: by the reddening or whitening of the face: by a sense of headache.[3]

Muhammad himself was initially in doubt as to the nature of these episodes, but was persuaded by his wife, Khadijah (a wealthy former widow and owner of a caravan), that they were "from God." Khadijah came from an Ebionite Christian background. Ebionites did not accept the letters of the apostle Paul. They observed the Old Testament dietary laws and viewed Jesus as a prophet, but not as God incarnate.

Recent studies have been published by Dr. Dede Korkut, a Turkish neurologist, in his book *Life Alert*. He demonstrates very convincingly that the underlying physiological source of Muhammad's experiences was the combined effect of hydrocephalus and epilepsy. The characteristics exhibited by individuals suffering from these conditions include episodes of sharp sensory hallucinations, recurrent dreams, distorted perceptions of reality, and impaired memory—

TABLE 5 Sample passages from the Noble Qur'an

Type	Excerpt	Sura
Pre-Islamic legend	"We covenanted with Abraham and Ismail that they should sanctify My House [the Ka'aba] for those who compass it round, or use it as a retreat, or bow, or prostrate themselves."	2:125
	"It has been revealed to me that a company of Jinns [genies, unseen spirits] listened (to the Qur'an). They said, 'We have really heard a wonderful Recital!' "	72:1
	"Behold! Safa and Marwa [little hills in Mecca] are among the Symbols of Allah. So if those who visit The House in the Season or at other times should compass them round, it is no sin in them."	2:158
Inaccurate biblical narrative	"And Noah called out to his son, who had separated himself (from the rest): 'O my son! embark with us, and be not with the Unbelievers!' . . . And the waves came between them, and the son was among those overwhelmed in the Flood."	11:42–43
	"Then, when (the son) [Ishmael] reached (the age of) (serious) work with him [Abraham], he said: 'O my son! I see in vision that I offer you in sacrifice.' "	37:102
	"The wife of Pharaoh said: '(Here is) a joy of the eye, for me and for you: do not slay him [Moses].' "	28:9
	"Pharaoh said: 'O Chiefs! no god do I know for you but myself: therefore, O Haman! light me a (kiln to bake bricks) out of clay, and build me a lofty Palace, that I may mount up to the god of Moses.' "	28:38
Fanciful tales	"They said: 'How can we talk to one who is a child in the cradle?' He [infant Jesus] said: 'I am indeed a servant of Allah: He has given me Revelation and made me a prophet.' "	19:29–30
	"And well ye knew those amongst you who transgressed in the matter of the Sabbath: We said to them: 'Be you apes, despised and rejected.' "	2:65
	"When We shook the Mount over them, as if it had been a canopy, and they thought it was going to fall on them . . ."	7:171

35

TABLE 5 (*continued*)

Type	Excerpt	Sura
	"But Allah caused him to die for a hundred years, then raised him up (again)."	2:259
	"Then Allah sent a raven, who scratched the ground, to show him how to hide the shame of his brother."	5:31
Repetition	"And it is He [Allah] who has power over all things."	5:120, etc.
	"He knows what you hide, and what you reveal, and He knows the (recompense) which you earn (by your deeds)."	6:3, etc.
	"Truly strong is the Grip (and Power) of your Lord."	85:12, etc.

exactly the types of behaviors that accompanied Muhammad's revelations.

The information that Muhammad recited during these episodes reflected a mixture of pre-Islamic legend, inaccurate and incomplete biblical narrative, fanciful tales, and repetitive recitation regarding the nature of a god labeled "Allah." Table 5 lists examples of the types of revelations common in the Noble Qur'an.

By merging known pre-Islamic legend with misunderstood biblical material, Muhammad was able to deliver a "scriptural-like" message directed specifically to and for the Arabic people. Muhammad became the "Arabian prophet," bringing Allah's final and definitive message to the world through those who would come to be known as the descendants of Ishmael.

PROPHETHOOD IN THE HOLY BIBLE

The early tribes of Arabia can be forgiven their gullibility in embracing Muhammad's claim. They possessed no standard for evaluating true prophethood. But today, we can readily go to the Scriptures in almost any major language to obtain an accurate description of the true prophets of Yahweh. Table 6 outlines those main characteristics, according to the Holy Bible.

The first three characteristics, shown in capital letters, are crucial in the determination of the true status of a biblical

TABLE 6 Characteristics of true prophets or true prophecy in the Holy Bible

Characteristic	Excerpt	Reference
SPOKE THE WORD FROM YAHWEH	"I [Yahweh] will put my words in his mouth."	Deut. 18:18
FORTHTELLING AND FORETELLING (PREDICTIVE), ALWAYS CORRECT	"If what a prophet proclaims in the name of the LORD does not take place or come true, that is a message the LORD has not spoken." [Note: "LORD" in large and small capital letters denotes the proper name of the biblical Triune God, Yahweh.]	Deut. 18:22
MESSAGE CENTERED ON THE CHRIST	"Indeed, all the prophets from Samuel on . . . have foretold these days [of Jesus Christ]."	Acts 3:24
Performed signs and visible miracles that glorify Yahweh	"But take this staff in your hand so you can perform miraculous signs with it."	Ex. 4:17
Received revelation in visions and dreams	"I reveal myself to him in visions, I speak to him in dreams."	Num. 12:6
Spoke in parables	"I spoke to the prophets, gave them many visions and told parables through them."	Hos. 12:10
Were set apart and sanctified, sometimes before birth	"Before you were born, I set you apart; I appointed you as a prophet to the nations."	Jer. 1:5
Were filled with the Holy Spirit	"His father Zechariah was filled with the Holy Spirit and prophesied."	Luke 1:67
Edified the church	"He who prophesies edifies the church."	I Cor. 14:4
Were under control	"The spirits of prophets are subject to the control of prophets. For God is not a God of disorder but of peace."	I Cor. 14:32

prophet. The prophet and the message he delivers must demonstrate all the qualities of Divine Truth in order to be considered the Word of the historical biblical God. The message will be pure Truth, the whole Truth, and nothing but the Truth. That message will be "Christocentric." Its main purpose will be to point to the Messiah, Jesus Christ, who is the ultimate Truth and complete Word of God. Any prophecies that predict future events unconditionally will come to pass inevitably and will be given with sufficient specific detail to make their fulfillment clear and prove their truthfulness. There is no compromise of these three parameters within the biblical prophetic model. The other characteristics listed may or may not be demonstrated by individual prophets. They reveal the general and acceptable peculiarities of prophets of Yahweh.

Note that within this list, or in the entire Holy Bible, the types of physical or physiological behaviors exhibited by Muhammad are never attributed to the true prophets. Those kinds of behaviors are described in only one place: the report of the demoniac healed by Jesus in Luke 9:37–43:

> The next day, when they came down from the mountain, a large crowd met him. A man in the crowd called out, "Teacher, I beg you to look at my son, for he is my only child. A spirit seizes him and he suddenly screams; it throws him into convulsions so that he foams at the mouth. It scarcely ever leaves him and is destroying him. I begged your disciples to drive it out, but they could not."
>
> "O unbelieving and perverse generation," Jesus replied, "how long shall I stay with you and put up with you? Bring your son here."

Even while the boy was coming, the demon threw him to the ground in a convulsion. But Jesus rebuked the evil spirit, healed the boy and gave him back to his father. And they were all amazed at the greatness of God.

The people of Arabia and foreigners among them were very familiar with the peculiarities of people overcome by evil spirits. For this reason many immediately considered Muhammad to be "possessed" and discarded his "revelations."

When we apply the table 6 categorical standards to Muhammad and his message, the result (table 7) is quite different. Muhammad attempted to frame his message in prophetic terms, but his understanding of the office was limited. Muhammad spent a great deal of time defending himself from charges of demonic possession, asserting his claim to authority, and pronouncing dire warnings to those who refused to believe in his revelation.

In the time of Muhammad, the Arab people were not equipped to evaluate his claims by any valid standard. They knew as little about true biblical Christianity as Muhammad did. So, slowly but surely, he developed a following, drawn by his compelling personality and strong character.

Historically, we know that he was forced to flee to Medina when resistance to him increased in Mecca. During this exile, the nature and tone of the Qur'anic revelations changed. Previously, he had attempted to show continuity with Jewish and Christian thought, but after his time in Medina, his message became more critical of Jewish and Christian populations, who had not embraced his message. He began referring to them as "infidels," and included them among the idolaters and pagans of the peninsula.

TABLE 7 Application of prophetic characteristics to Muhammad

Characteristic	Excerpt	Reference
SPEAKS WORD FROM ALLAH	"In the name of Allah, Most Gracious, Most Merciful . . ."	Beginning of every Sura
PROPHESIES BY FORTHTELLING ONLY	"Those who purchase Unbelief at the price of faith . . . will have a grievous punishment."	Sura 3:177
HIS MESSAGE CENTERED ON QUR'AN AND PROPHET	"What then is the matter with them, that they do not believe? And when the Qur'an is read to them, they do not fall prostrate."	Sura 84:20–21
	"Verily this is the word of a most honorable Messenger, Endued with Power, with rank before the Lord of the Throne, with authority there."	Sura 81:19–21
Signs: verses of Qur'an	"When Our Signs are rehearsed to him [the unbeliever], he says, 'Tales of the Ancients!' "	Sura 83:13
Revelatory means: visions and unusual psycho-physical behaviors	"And, (O people!) your Companion [Muhammad] is not one possessed; And without doubt he saw him [Gabriel] in the clear horizon."	Sura 81:22
Used similitudes	"If anyone assigns partners to Allah, he is as if he had fallen from heaven and been snatched up by birds."	Sura 22:31
Called from Arab nation	"Allah conferred a great favor on the Believers when he sent among them a Messenger from among themselves."	Sura 3:164
Filled with agitation	"Then Allah's Apostle returned with the inspiration and with his heart beating severely. Then he went to Khadija bint Khywailid and said, 'Cover me! Cover me!' They covered him till his fear was over."	Sahih al-Bukhari, Hadith 1.1.3
Criticized the church	"You People of the Book! Why do you clothe truth with falsehood, and conceal the Truth . . . ?"	Sura 3:71
Not under control	"He fell down unconscious on the ground with both his eyes [open] towards the sky."	Hadith 6:448

His mission became increasingly militaristic. He eventually returned to Mecca as a victorious conqueror and set upon the task of succeeding where Jesus had "failed"—to establish the kingdom of Allah on earth, based on the strict law of the "one true religion," Islam.

THE EXALTATION OF MUHAMMAD

Although Muhammad made no claims to sinless superiority regarding his status as a prophet, he was increasingly mythologized as Islam spread. The desire for the appearance of a "prophet like Moses" had captured the imagination of the growing Muslim community, and this image was cast upon Muhammad.

Writes Ibn Warraq, in his introduction to *Origins of the Koran:*

Much influenced by the Rabbinic accounts, the early Muslim community took Moses as an exemplum, and then a portrait of Muhammad emerged, but only gradually and in response to the needs of a religious community. It was anxious to establish Muhammad's credentials as a prophet on the Mosaic model; this evidently meant there had to be a Holy Scripture, which would be seen as testimony to his prophethood. Another gradual development was the emergence of the idea of the Arabian origins of Islam. To this end, there was elaborated the concept of a sacred language, Arabic.[4]

The assembly of the Noble Qur'an and its elevation as the final word of God, placed above the previous Scriptures in value and authority, were essential to this effort. Following this was the exaltation of Muhammad as a larger-than-life figure, endowed with traits and attributes surpassing those of any other prophet.

In a contemporary online article entitled "Twelve Proofs That Muhammad Is a True Prophet," by Shaykh 'Abdul Rahman 'Abdul Khaliq, originally published by the Islamic Association of North America and at the Internet site www.islaam.com, the following points are listed as verifications of Muhammad's prophethood (condensed from the original article for easy reference):

"Proofs" of Muhammad as a Prophet

- He was illiterate for his entire life.
- He had no religious knowledge or training.
- The biblical stories in the Qur'an are exact and in precise detail.
- All of his prophecies have been fulfilled exactly.
- Qur'anic Arabic is eloquent and clear.
- He demonstrated a perfect life of striving for the hereafter.
- His believers would sacrifice and ransom to see him.
- His biography has been preserved like no other throughout history.
- His believers follow him in all details of life.
- He is loved, honored, respected, and obeyed like no other prophet.
- His followers suffer great persecution.
- Qur'anic laws apply to all human activity.
- Qur'anic teaching on human character and manners is exemplary.
- The Creator sent the law and religion of Islam.

Few characteristics, if any, on this list remind us of true biblical prophets. Most of the "proofs" listed are inconsequential, untrue, or outrageous. They have nothing to do with any previously known prophetic attributes and show a marked propensity toward the practical deification of Muhammad.

The only attribute appearing on both this and the biblical prophet list is the fulfillment of predictive prophecy. Authors Norman L. Geisler and Abdul Saleeb, in their volume *Answering Islam,* note that the suras often cited as being predictive prophecies are those promising victory to Islamic troops. Passages quoted as foretelling specific future events, such as Sura 30:2–4 regarding the battle at Issus, and Sura 89:2 warning of ten years of persecution, simply do not meet the standards of historic specificity or veracity in order to be regarded as authentic.

But, even more importantly, Geisler and Saleeb continue, "Muhammad never offered his alleged prophecy as a proof of his prophethood."[5] Nor did Muhammad offer any signs or miracles as evidence of his prophethood. The Noble Qur'an repeatedly asserts that Muhammad refused to perform any miracles, including predictive prophecy. He pointed to the Noble Qur'an as his only "sign" of prophetic office. Yet a later Hadith records Muhammad as saying:

I have been granted excellence over the other prophets in six things: the earth has been made a mosque for me, with its soil declared pure; booty has been made lawful for me; I have been given victory through the inspiring of awe at the distance of a month's journey; I have been given permission to intercede; I have been sent to all mankind; and the prophets have been sealed with me.[6]

THE MAKING OF A LEGEND

Fueled by these kinds of claims, stories about Muhammad continued to build up over time. According to Imam an-Nawawi's article "Prophet Muhammad's Miracles" at www.islaam.com, Muhammad performed such feats as

> splitting of the moon, water flowing from between his fingers, increasing the quality of food and water, the glorification of the food, the palm tree yearning for him, stones greeting him, the talking of the poisoned leg [of roasted sheep], trees walking towards him, two trees that were far apart coming together and then parting again, the barren [and therefore dry] sheep giving milk, his returning the eye of Qatidah bin an-Nu'man to its place with his hand after it had slipped out, his spitting lightly into the eye of Ali when it had become inflamed and its being cured almost immediately, his wiping the leg of 'Abdullah bin 'Atiq whereupon he was immediately cured.[7]

Some of these events show superficial similarity to the biblical miracles of Jesus Christ, or of his apostles. Most are fanciful tales bearing no resemblance to any truly prophetic deed. There seems to be almost a childlike naiveté in ascribing them to Muhammad, a sort of one-upmanship designed to prove that "our prophet's better than yours."

Muhammad was eventually endowed with sinlessness and perfection. In an online article at www.islaam.com entitled

"The Prophet Muhammad's Conduct and Morals as an Evidence of His Prophethood," by Dr. Abdul Radhi Muhammad Abdul Mohsen, we read that the three "fields of moral perfection that are reliable proofs of prophethood" are the Perfection of Qualities, the Virtues of the Prophet's Speech, and the Virtues of the Prophet's Deeds. In addition, "Never before the advent of Muhammad . . . was the moral perfection an evidence of prophethood."[8]

It is true that these kinds of characteristics are never cited as proofs of prophethood. There is a reason for this. Moral perfection is unattainable by any mere human beings, including prophets. Perfection is an attribute of deity, not humanity. Man has an intense inner desire to worship perfection. If he has not encountered it through divine revelation, he will create it, often in his own image, in order to direct his adoration.

Although not embraced by orthodox Islam, there exists a popular "veneration of Muhammad to the extent of almost deifying him."[9] In addition, "the adulation of Muhammad by Muslims parallels the Christian adoration of Jesus"[10]; and "for all practical purposes Muhammad himself is the Muslim Christ."[11]

Muslims have given Muhammad additional titles, much like those given to Allah. They include "the Forgiver," "the Raiser of the Dead," "the Perfect," the Interceder," "the Holy Spirit," "the Lord of Two Worlds," and "the glory of the Arabs."[12] "Islam denies the need of Christ as Mediator, only to substitute Mohammed as a mediator, without an incarnation, without an atonement, and without demand for a change of character."[13] This is a hollow anointing— an Arab "messiah" without any power to save.

45

IMITATION AND APPROPRIATION

When a "leader-god" is established by men, followers often attempt to increase their piety by imitating the leader's every observable deed and practice. Significance is assigned to the most tedious tasks. Muslim theologian Al-Ghazali writes in *Ihya ulum ad-din* (*Revival of Religious Sciences*):

> Know that the key to happiness is to follow the sunna [Muhammad's actions] and to imitate the Messenger of God in all his coming and going, his movement and rest, in his way of eating, his attitude, his sleep and his talk. . . . God has said: "What the messenger has brought—accept it, and what he has prohibited—refrain from it!" (59:7) That means, you have to sit while putting on trousers, and to stand when winding a turban, and to begin with the right foot when putting on shoes.[14]

Devout Muslims have embraced this imitative ritual, going so far as to teach zealous followers the method Muhammad used to trim his toenails. All of this is done in the tragically mistaken hope that through these actions one can gain greater favor from Allah and be considered more virtuous.

Many practices eventually take on the distinctive aura of superstition. Implements or behaviors come to be regarded as special charms, possessing their own merit and power. Followers merge the new rituals with old familiar pagan practices, creating what may be referred to as "popular" or "folk Islam." Samuel Zwemer discusses this in great detail in part two of *Islam and the Cross:* "Many doctrines and practices of popular Islam find their explanation only in a survival of the animism of ancient Arabia or were incorporated from many heathen sources in the spread of the faith."[15]

It may be helpful at this point to look at characteristics that the Holy Bible uses to describe those who do not speak in the name of Yahweh (see table 8).

Writes Edward J. Young in his book *My Servants the Prophets:*

Two kinds of prophets existed side by side in Israel—the true and the false. The true came forth with a message from Jehovah, a message for the benefit of the nation. The false uttered a message of human origination, and consequently, one which could not meet the deep needs of the people and which could not be for its ultimate good. Any serious attempt to account for the origin and nature of prophecy in Israel must take full account of these two groups and of the profound gulf which separated them. The one was from man; the other from God.[16]

Regarding false prophetic messages, Young continues:

Whether that message was the direct product of the inspiration of a lying spirit or whether it was the product of his own heart—and there seem to have been instances of both—the false prophet proclaimed a message that was not in accord with the truth because he had not been sent by God, and the Word of God had not been placed in his mouth.[17]

47

TABLE 8 Characteristics of prophets of other gods or those who bear false messages

Characteristic	Excerpt	Reference
Follow unknown gods	"If a prophet, or one who foretells by dreams, appears among you and announces to you a miraculous sign . . . and he says, 'Let us follow other gods' (gods you have not known) 'and let us worship them, you must not listen.' "	Deut. 13:1–3
Frenzied worship practices	"So they shouted louder and slashed themselves with swords and spears, as was their custom, until their blood flowed."	1 Kings 18:28
Empowered by lying spirit	"The LORD has put a lying spirit in the mouths of all these prophets of yours. The LORD has decreed disaster for you."	1 Kings 22:23
Teach lies	"The prophets who teach lies are the tail."	Isa. 9:15
Follow idols	"The prophets prophesied by Baal, following worthless idols."	Jer. 2:8
Word is not in them	"The prophets are but wind and the word is not in them."	Jer. 5:13
Practice deceit	"Prophets and priests alike, all practice deceit."	Jer. 6:13
Not appointed by Yahweh	"The prophets are prophesying lies in my name. I have not sent them or appointed them or spoken to them. They are prophesying to you false visions, divinations, idolatries and the delusions of their own minds."	Jer. 14:14
Evil and unjust	"The prophets follow an evil course and use their power unjustly. Both prophet and priest are godless."	Jer. 23:10–11
Lead astray	"They prophesied by Baal and led my people Israel astray."	Jer. 23:13
Commit adultery	"They commit adultery and live a lie. They strengthen the hands of evildoers."	Jer. 23:14
Give false hope	"They fill you with false hopes. They speak visions from their own minds, not from the mouth of the LORD."	Jer. 23:16

48

TABLE 8 (*continued*)

Characteristic	Excerpt	Reference
Get people to forget Yahweh	"They think the dreams they tell one another will make my people forget my name, just as their fathers forgot my name through Baal worship."	Jer. 23:27
Steal words from each other	"I am against the prophets who steal from one another words supposedly from me."	Jer. 23:30
Give one's own word	"Every man's own word becomes his oracle and so you distort the words of the living God."	Jer. 23:36
Become fools	"A sword against her false prophets! They will become fools."	Jer. 50:36
Do not expose sin	"The visions of your prophets were false and worthless; they did not expose your sin to ward off your captivity. The oracles they gave you were false and misleading."	Lam. 2:14
Prophesy from own imagination, wear charms	"I am against your magic charms with which you ensnare people like birds and I will tear them from your arms; I will set free the people that you ensnare like birds. I will tear off your veils and save my people from your hands, and they will no longer fall prey to your power. Then you will know that I am the LORD."	Ezek. 13:20–21
Arrogant	"Her prophets are arrogant; they are treacherous men."	Zeph. 3:4
Come in sheep's clothing	"Watch out for false prophets. They come to you in sheep's clothing, but inwardly they are ferocious wolves. By their fruit you will recognize them."	Matt. 7:15
Many will appear at end of age	"At that time many will turn away from the faith and will betray and hate each other, and many false prophets will appear and deceive many people."	Matt. 24:10–11
Perform signs	"For false Christs and false prophets will appear and perform great signs and miracles to deceive even the elect—if that were possible. See, I have told you ahead of time."	Matt. 24:24–25

49

TABLE 8 *(continued)*

Characteristic	Excerpt	Reference
May be spoken well of	"Woe to you when all men speak well of you, for that is how their fathers treated the false prophets."	Luke 6:26
Introduce heresies	"But there were also false prophets among the people. . . . They will secretly introduce destructive heresies, even denying the sovereign Lord who bought them—bringing swift destruction on themselves."	2 Peter 2:1
Do not acknowledge Jesus Christ	"Every spirit that does not acknowledge Jesus is not from God."	1 John 4:3

PROPHET IN CONFLICT

Islam goes to great lengths to try to place Muhammad within the ranks of the inspired biblical prophets, even going so far as to use incredible redaction. Attempts have been made to retranslate portions of the Holy Bible to include prophecies of Muhammad's ascendancy, reinterpret passages to reflect the rise of Islam, and even rewrite the words of Jesus Christ to deliver testimony of Muhammad. None of these techniques has been taken seriously by biblical scholars; they simply lack any exegetical merit.

So Islam has chosen the next best route: to establish its own set of prophethood parameters, based on the exalted standard of a mythologized Muhammad, and to defend it with circular reasoning.

There is no doubt that Muhammad's message was in conflict with orthodox biblical Christianity. It doesn't matter whether this was due to his ignorance of the truths of biblical faith and its Holy Scriptures, or due to overt antagonism toward them. It doesn't matter if he made these proclamations under the influence of a hallucinogenic medical condi-

50

tion or if he deliberately set out to deceive. It doesn't matter if his "heart was in the right place" and he delivered his message with the intention of unifying the Arab tribes and imposing order among them through religious homogenization, or if he was a megalomaniac with the sole desire of subjugating his people under his own charismatic personality.

What does matter is that the message was not Truth and the messenger was not true.

The biblical standard for excellent personal character is found in Jesus Christ, the epitome of righteousness (see table 9). In addition to his divine attributes, Jesus Christ displays excellency in all the finest characteristics of humanity. This is the portrait of perfect morality. It provides the standard for evaluating any other such claims.

It should be understood that Jesus Christ, because of his special status as a fully divine and fully human being, reveals perfection within his human nature by virtue of his divinity. Muhammad, on the other hand, never asserted divinity, although the Noble Qur'an asserts that Muhammad stands "on an exalted standard of character" (Sura 68:4). Therefore, we are justified in exploring whether or not this claim is true.

TABLE 9   The personality of Jesus Christ

Characteristic	Excerpt	Reference
Altogether lovely	"His mouth is sweetness itself; he is altogether lovely."	Song 5:16
Holy	"So the holy one to be born will be called the Son of God."	Luke 1:35
Righteous	"My righteous servant will justify many, and he will bear their iniquities."	Isa. 53:11
Good	"Jesus replied, 'There is only One who is good.' "	Matt. 19:17
Faithful	"The one who calls you is faithful, and he will do it."	1 Thess. 5:24

51

TABLE 9 *(continued)*

Characteristic	Excerpt	Reference
True	"... that we may know him who is true. And we are in him who is true— even in his Son Jesus Christ."	1 John 5:20
Just	"I judge only as I hear, and my judgment is just."	John 5:30
Guileless	"He committed no sin, and no deceit was found in his mouth."	1 Peter 2:22
Sinless	"God made him who had no sin to be sin for us."	2 Cor. 5:21
Perfect	"... the precious blood of Christ, a lamb without blemish or defect."	1 Peter 1:19
Innocent	"[Judas said,] 'I have betrayed innocent blood.' "	Matt. 27:4
Blameless	"Such a high priest meets our need— one who is holy, blameless, pure."	Heb. 7:26
Resisting temptation	"Jesus said to him, 'Away from me, Satan!' "	Matt. 4:10
Obedient to Yahweh	"I always do what pleases him [the Father]."	John 8:29
Gentle and humble	"I am gentle and humble in heart, and you will find rest for your souls."	Matt. 11:29
Merciful	"... in order that he might become a merciful and faithful high priest in service to God ..."	Heb. 2:17
Patient and longsuffering	"... Christ Jesus might display his unlimited patience ..."	1 Tim. 1:16
Compassionate	"Jesus went throughout Galilee, teaching in their synagogues, preaching the good news of the kingdom, and healing every disease and sickness."	Matt. 4:23
Loving	"Greater love has no one than this, that he lay down his life for his friends."	John 15:13
Poor	"Though he was rich, yet for your sakes he became poor."	2 Cor. 8:9
Humble	"He humbled himself and became obedient to death."	Phil. 2:8
Selfless	"... yet not my will, but yours be done."	Luke 22:42
Forgiving	"Jesus said, 'Father, forgive them, for they do not know what they are doing.' "	Luke 23:34

THE CHARACTER OF MUHAMMAD

In order to fully understand Muhammad, it is helpful to have a better grasp of Arab personality and culture in general. Georges Houssney, in his article entitled "Arab Character" in the June 1989 issue of *ReachOut* magazine, enumerates the following traits:

- Pessimistic
- Disrespectful toward authority
- Careless and disorganized
- Imprecise in measuring time blocks
- Temperamental
- Traditional and conformist
- Courageous
- Loyal
- Prone to place high value on honor and pride
- Vengeful
- Hospitable
- Romantic
- Intuitive and spontaneous

He explains these attributes in terms of the Arabic understanding of deity, the hardships of desert life, and the pervasive belief in "fate" that leaves the Arab few, if any, choices in life. Muhammad was molded by this cultural worldview. His character and message are a clear reflection of the Arab mind-set.

Many books recount the biographical details of Muhammad's life. Some are listed in the resource pages of this volume. One of the most complete is Ibn Warraq's *The Quest for the Historical Muhammad*. The shared conclusions of

53

these works, summarized below, present a clear picture of the historical Muhammad.

Muhammad was, at his core, ambitious and deliberate. The claim to prophethood, based on periodic seizure-like episodes, gave him status and authority among the Arab people. The pronouncement of a divine book sealed that authority.

As his power grew, so did his desire for greater control. He used all the means at his disposal to subdue and conquer. Raiding caravans, raising a militia, taking captives, ordering public executions—all were legitimate for him, since he was the "chosen messenger" of Allah. While there is no doubt that he could be charming and charismatic, his nature was one of domination. The picture that emerges from biographical data, *even from Muslim scholars,* is not flattering. Ibn Warraq explains:

[The] character attributed to Mohammed in the biography of Ibn Ishaq is exceedingly unfavorable. In order to gain his ends he recoils from no expedient, and he approves of similar unscrupulousness on the part of his adherents, when exercised in his interest. He profits to the utmost from the chivalry of the Meccans, but rarely requites it with the like. He organizes assassinations and wholesale massacres. His career as tyrant of Medina is that of a robber chief, whose political economy consists in securing and dividing plunder, the distribution of the latter being at times carried out on principles which fail to satisfy his follower's ideas of justice. He is himself an unbridled libertine and encourages the same passion in his followers. For whatever he does he is prepared to plead the express authorization of the deity. It is, however, impossible to find any doctrine which he is not prepared to abandon in order to secure a political end.[18]

Muhammad was a very human being, full of passions and desires, sins, and even some virtues. But he was not a true prophet of the God of the universe. His message, remarkable though it may have been, was the product of a highly creative but chaotic mind. Intoxicated by political power and supplemented by the acquisition of spiritual authority, he transformed the Arabian peninsula and its people into a formidable theocratic entity.

The territorial and religious fanaticism inherent in Qur'anic Islam fueled a massive militaristic movement that managed to encompass a large portion of the Middle East, Asia, northern Africa, and southern Spain in an astonishingly short time. History confirms that conquest by the sword has always been Islam's primary method of propagating its message. Muslims make no apology for this, for the Qur'anic mandate to overcome and subdue other populations and bring them under Islamic shari'ah law is clear and compelling. Those who strive for this domination—engaging in the accurate interpretation of "jihad"—are fulfilling the ultimate goal of Islam: the establishment of the kingdom of Allah on earth.

This is the truth about Islam.

"A PRAYER FOR THE MUSLIM WORLD"
(CONTINUED)

. . . Hasten the day
of religious freedom
in Turkey, Arabia, Iran,
Iraq, Afghanistan,
and North Africa.
Send forth reapers
where the harvest is ripe,
and faithful plowmen
to break furrows
in lands still neglected.
May the tribes of Africa
and Malaysia
not fall a prey to Islam
but be won for Christ.
Bless the ministry of healing
in every hospital,
and the ministry of love
at every church and mission.
May all Muslim children
in mission schools
be led to Christ
and accept him
as their personal Savior . . .

3

JESUS CHRIST IN QUR'ANIC
AND BIBLICAL THOUGHT

But what about you?' he
asked. 'Who do you say I am?' " (Matt. 16:15). It seems such
a simple question, yet the answer is the hinge of eternity for
man. Who, indeed, is Jesus Christ?

Simon Peter answered simply and accurately, "You are
the Christ, the Son of the living God" (Matt. 16:16). By
Peter's words, the true and divine nature of Jesus Christ was
identified and affirmed.

Focus is generally placed on the word *you*. But there is
another very important word in this question. Jesus asks,
"*Who* do you say I am?"

SONSHIP DEFINED

One does not strive to be a son—one is, or one is not.
Becoming a son may occur through natural generation or
through legal adoption. In the former, the son shares the
genetic characteristics of his parents, good and bad. In the
latter, the son is "chosen" and lovingly brought into a fam-

ily, with all the attendant privileges and responsibilities of family name and membership. In neither case does the son have anything to say, or do, in the matter. Admission to sonship has no requirements to be fulfilled. A son is who he is.

All human sons, sharing the genetic characteristics of their biological parents, are, in the biblical sense, "begotten." Their natures are determined by inheritance. These thoroughly human natures may be altered, for better or worse, by the environments in which they mature.

So what does this have to do with Jesus Christ?

ONLY BEGOTTEN SON OF THE FATHER

The Holy Bible maintains that Jesus is the "only begotten Son" of God the Father (John 3:16 KJV). Yet we know that God is Spirit and that his nature displays divine attributes unique to him and not found in man. How can we understand God's "begetting" of a human Son?

Human parents, of course, come together in physical intimacy to initiate conception, but the Godhead initiated the birth of his Son by the intimate spiritual power of the third Person of his own Being, the Holy Spirit. The miracle of the incarnation of the Son was a singular supernatural event, occurring in the human dimensions of time and space, through the infinite and eternal power of the biblical Triune God.

God the Father chose the young girl, Mary of Nazareth, to bear the Holy Child. Her assent was humble: "May it be to me as you have said" (Luke 1:38). Jesus Christ was born, receiving Mary's fully human nature and the lineage of King David. Completing the miracle, Jesus Christ also inherited the divine nature or substance of his Heavenly Father.

58

How can this be? How can perfect divinity and imperfect humanity be present in one Being?

Because the Father is holy, sin cannot abide in his presence. Neither can it endure in the Person of his Son. Therefore, the corruption of original sin resulting from Adam's fall was never found in Jesus. He bears the human image in its best and most perfect sense. All the finest and highest attributes of humanity are found in him, uncorrupted and unblemished.

THE ISLAMIC VIEW OF JESUS CHRIST

Islam honors Jesus Christ only as a prophet and apostle. Although Muslims maintain that he is the point of intersection for Islam and Christianity, they do not recognize his unique identity as the divine Son of Yahweh. Their image of him, therefore, is an incomplete one. When Muslims are asked, "Who do you say Jesus is?" they can only reply either with a limited explanation of his roles or (as when describing Allah) with descriptions of what he is *not* (see table 10).

TABLE 10   The nature of Christ in the Noble Qur'an

Description	Excerpt	Sura
Not God	"In blasphemy indeed are those that say that God is Christ."	5:17
Not the Son of God	"The Christians call Christ the Son of Allah. . . . Allah's curse be on them."	9:30
	"It is not befitting to (the majesty of) Allah that He should beget a son . . ."	19:35
Not possessing divine attributes	"You [Allah] know what is in my [Jesus'] heart, though I do not know what is in Yours."	5:116
Not crucified	"They did not kill him [Jesus], nor crucified him."	4:157
Like Adam	"The similitude of Jesus before Allah is as that of Adam."	3:59

The concept of Allah provides the lens through which Jesus is viewed in Islam. Because Allah requires no mediator between himself and man, Jesus Christ is unnecessary as an intercessor. Because man is able to achieve personal righteousness through law, Jesus Christ's mission to provide vicarious atonement for man's sin is meaningless. Because Allah does not desire to make himself known to man in any tangible immanent way, he has no reason to become man, nor will he share his glory with any other being or personality. Because he is not regarded as a "father" in any sense of the word, he has no son, begotten or adopted.

DENIAL OF CRUCIFIXION

The central biblical testimony regarding Jesus' crucifixion is denied in the Noble Qur'an. On the islaminfo.com Web site, a number of articles deal with the Islamic view of Jesus Christ. One, entitled "Jesus, on whom be peace, in the Glorious Qur'an," states that to save Jesus from death on the cross, "Allah rescued Jesus and raised him to Himself."[1] This is taken from Sura 4:158 and is explained in the footnote on this sura in the Ali text of the Noble Qur'an: "The Qur'anic teaching is that Christ was not crucified nor killed by the Jews, notwithstanding certain apparent circumstances which produced that illusion in the minds of some of his enemies . . . and that he was taken up to God."[2]

Islamic traditions written by authoritative commentators explain this rescue in various ways. Wahab (from whom came the branch of Islam known as Wahabism, prevalent in modern-day Saudi Arabia) tells us that Allah "cast the likeness of Jesus upon him who had betrayed Him, and his name was Judas. And they crucified him in His stead, and they thought that they crucified Jesus. Then Allah made Jesus to die for three hours, and then raised Him up to heaven. . . ."

Makatal, however, said that the religious authorities had appointed a spy to watch Jesus, and Allah made that man resemble him. The spy was mistakenly crucified instead of Jesus. Katada relates that Jesus asked for a willing volunteer among his companions to die in his place and that a man named Ashua (common form of *Joshua,* or *Jesus*), son of Kandir, offered to give himself and was crucified.

None of these stories has any verifying historical sources, written or oral, and are not supported by the biblically reported behavior of Jesus' intimate friends and family members who witnessed his death.

The online article continues, "Allah will cause Jesus to descend again, at which time Jesus will confirm his true teachings and everyone will believe in him as he is and as the Qur'an teaches about him." According to Islam, Jesus will then die and be buried in the tomb reserved for him near the resting place of Muhammad.

Other descriptive passages about Jesus Christ are listed in table 11. It is immediately apparent that quite a bit of the information concerning Jesus Christ provided in the Noble Qur'an is very different from what we read in the Holy Bible. Detailed accounts of the nativity and his teaching ministry are completely absent, as well as the retelling of his parables and testimony regarding his miracles. He is reported to have been given the "gospel" (*injil*), but we are not specifically told what that is, except for the frequent assertion that he speaks the word of Allah. There is no mention of the good news declaring man's reconciliation with Yahweh

61

TABLE 11   The Person of Jesus Christ in the Noble Qur'an

Description	Excerpt	Sura
Apostle of Allah	"Christ Jesus . . . was (no more than) a Messenger of Allah."	4:171
Apostle to Israel	". . . a Messenger to the Children of Israel . . .	3:49–51
Christ (Messiah)	"His name will be Christ Jesus, the son of Mary, held in honor in this world and the Hereafter."	3:45
Prophet	". . . and Jesus and Elias: all in the ranks of the Righteous [Prophets]."	6:85
Miraculous conception	"[Mary] said: 'O my Lord! how shall I have a son when no man has touched me?' He said: 'Even so: Allah creates what He wills.' "	3:47
Born under a palm tree	"And the pains of childbirth drove her [Mary] to the trunk of a palm tree."	19:23
Speaks as an infant	" 'How can we talk to one who is a child in the cradle?' He [infant Jesus] said: 'I am indeed a servant of Allah.' "	19:29–30
A mercy	"(We wish) to appoint him [Jesus] as a Sign to men and a Mercy from Us."	19:21
Sign of judgment	"And [Jesus] shall be a Sign (for the coming) of the Hour (of Judgment)."	43:61
Servant	"He [Jesus] was no more than a servant."	43:59
Servant raised to honor	"They are (but)servants raised to honor. They do not speak before He speaks, and they act (in all things) by His command."	21:26–27
Word of Allah	". . . His Word, which He bestowed on Mary . . ."	4:171
Spirit from Allah	". . . and a Spirit proceeding from Him . . ."	4:171
To be obeyed	"He [Jesus] said . . . 'fear Allah and obey me.' "	43:63
Miracle-worker by Allah's permission	"You [Jesus] brought forth the dead by My [Allah's] leave."	5:110
Makes clay birds fly	"I make for you out of clay, as it were, the figure of a bird, and breathe into it, and it becomes a bird by Allah's leave."	3:49
Spoke only by command of Allah	" 'Never said I to them anything except what You commanded me to say.' "	5:117

TABLE 11 *(continued)*

Description	Excerpt	Sura
Given the gospel	"We sent him the Gospel: therein was guidance and light, and confirmation of the Law."	5:46
Forerunner of Muhammad	" '. . . giving Glad Tidings of a Messenger to come after me [Jesus], whose name shall be Ahmad.' "	61:6

through Jesus' sacrificial atonement, in fulfillment of the Old Testament law and prophecy.

There is simply no theological or historical connection between the Islamic prophet Jesus as presented in the Noble Qur'an and the Savior of the world, Jesus Christ, revealed in the Holy Bible. The Jesus described by Muhammad is merely a caricature of the real biblical Christ. By stripping away Jesus' glory, Muhammad smoothed the way for his own "messianic" aspirations. Whether he did this ignorantly or intentionally is irrelevant; the damage has been done.

ISLAM'S PROPHET JESUS

Sura 19:19 states that Gabriel announced to Mary "the gift of a holy son." According to Ali's commentary on this sura, "his [Jesus'] mission was to bring solace and salvation to the repentant." In Islamic theology, granting salvation is the prerogative of Allah alone. It is curious that Ali's commentary grants this ability to Jesus Christ.

The accounts of the miraculous conception of Jesus Christ are also interesting. In Sura 66:12 we read, "We breathed into [her body] of Our spirit. . . ." Sura 3:59 states: "[Allah] created him [Jesus] from dust." Sura 3:47 tells us that "He [Allah] but says to it 'Be' and it is!" These passages are written to support the Islamic view of Jesus as a created human being and to counter the idea of him as a begotten Son of God. Although the descriptions are confusing, it is remarkable that the conception of no other prophet is discussed in as much detail in the Noble Qur'an as that of Jesus Christ.

Mary's betrothed husband, Joseph, is conspicuously absent from the Qur'anic accounts. According to the Holy Bible, he played a strong role in the protection of Mary and Jesus, but Joseph's testimony regarding divine guidance in dreams is entirely missing from the Noble Qur'an.

Jesus is the only prophet in Islam who is described as playing a major role in "the next world." In Islamic eschatology, Jesus Christ will return as an end-times military figure establishing Muslim political power over a vast earthly kingdom. Although this is cited by Islamic commentators as proof that Islam "honors" Jesus above all other prophets, with the exception of Muhammad, it is a hollow claim. For this apocalyptic Jesus is only the harbinger of the earthly "global civilization" of Islam, not the righteous Messiah of the world.

BIBLICAL MEANING OF *MESSIAH*

The fact that the Noble Qur'an uses the title *Messiah* or "Christ" to refer to Jesus is interpreted by some as a tacit approval of Jesus as a Savior. But let's examine this term carefully. "The word Messiah is the English transliteration of the Hebrew term mashiach, which means 'anointed.' "[3] The word has gone through a connotative evolution, as language often does. At first, it was applied to anyone anointed with ceremonial oil upon the assumption of a religious office. Most often, this office was that of prophet, priest, or king. Over time, the term became synonymous with those offices.

The word *mashiach* was translated into two separate Greek words when the Hellenization of the Middle East occurred and the Septuagint was produced from the Hebrew Scriptures. Transliterated (for linguistic accuracy), it was rendered *Messias*. Translated (for connotative accuracy), it was rendered *Christos*.

By the time of the Roman occupation of Palestine, the term was interpreted in light of specific Old Testament prophecies foretelling the advent of a particular individual, who would assume all three major offices—prophet, priest, and king—*simultaneously*.

The Messiah, then, was an ideal figure who embodied the hopes of the godly, patriotic Jew of the time. He would be a descendant of David and Solomon. He would be uniquely wise and knowledgeable, upright, courageous, and patriotic, loyally devoted to God. God's power would back Him, and God's wisdom would guide Him so that he could overthrow Israel's enemies and establish God's kingdom of justice, truth, and peace, wherein the Jewish people would worship and obey the one true God, and enjoy permanent prosperity and happiness.[4]

That, basically, is what the Messiah was in the minds of those who were looking for him when Jesus appeared on the scene.

THE ISLAMIC MEANING OF *MESSIAH*

Muslims translate the word *Messias* as "El Messih." Its etymology is traced to the Arabic root *sah*, which means "to wander or go on a pilgrimage." Turn-of-the-century missionary Samuel Zwemer, who spent 25 years in fellowship and communication with Muslims in Arabia, writes in *The Muslim Christ* that "it is the intensive form of that root [*sah*]. . . . Jesus was the leader of wanderers, 'Imam al sa'yihim.' "[5]

Zwemer notes that in Kamoos Fairozabadi's Arabic dictionary, the Arabic root *Masaha* ("to anoint") is given for *Messias*, but the entry explains that "this name was given to Jesus Christ because He was often on journeys, and did not spend His days in one place."[6] Thus, when readers of the Noble Qur'an see the terms *Messiah* and *Christ* employed as titles for Jesus, those terms do not have the same meanings for Muslims as they do for biblical Christians.

It is clear from the passages in table 12 that Jesus Christ is in full possession of the divine nature and endowed with characteristics ascribed only to Yahweh. He accepted the worship of followers and affirmed his inheritance as the Son. Many, many biblical passages attest to this, in addition to the many Old Testament messianic prophecies, which are fulfilled by the events of his earthly life. There is no question regarding this issue among those adhering to orthodox, historical biblical Christianity.

INCARNATIONAL CHRISTOLOGY

The doctrine of the two-natured Christ—true God and true man in one Person—is called "classical incarnational Christology." It is, admittedly, not an easy concept for the human intelligence to comprehend. "Any historical fact of transcendent significance such as the event of the incarnation must inevitably require the language of metaphysics if men are to explain it theologically," says Robert L.

TABLE 12   The nature of Jesus Christ in the Holy Bible

Description	Excerpt	Reference
God, in fullness	"For in Christ all the fullness of the Deity lives in bodily form."	Col. 2:9
God, in unity	" 'I [Jesus] and the Father are one.' "	John 10:30
God, in equality	". . . who, being in the form of God, did not consider it robbery to be equal with God."	Phil. 2:6 NKJV
God, in sovereignty	"Thomas said to him [Jesus], 'My Lord and my God!' "	John 20:28
God, in glory	". . . the blessed hope—the glorious appearing of our great God and Savior, Jesus Christ."	Titus 2:13
God, in the flesh	"According to the flesh, Christ came, who is over all, the eternally blessed God."	Rom. 9:5 NKJV
God, in eternity	"He is before all things, and in him all things hold together."	Col. 1:17
Only begotten Son of God	"For God so loved the world that he gave his only begotten Son, that whoever believes in Him should not perish, but have everlasting life."	John 3:16 NKJV
	". . . the glory as of the only begotten of the Father, full of grace and truth."	John 1:14 NKJV
	"The only begotten Son, who is in the bosom of the Father, He has declared Him."	John 1:18 NKJV
	"He who does not believe is condemned already, because he has not believed in the name of the only begotten Son of God."	John 3:18 NKJV
	"God has sent His only begotten Son into the world, that we might live through him."	1 John 4:9 NKJV
	" 'Tell us if You are the Christ, the Son of God!' Jesus said to him, 'It is as you said.' "	Matt. 26:63– 64 NKJV
Lord of glory	". . . the faith of our Lord Jesus Christ, the Lord of glory . . ."	James 2:1 NKJV
Image of God	". . . who [Jesus] being the brightness of His [Yahweh's] glory and the express image of His person . . ."	Heb. 1:3 NKJV

67

TABLE 12 *(continued)*

Description	Excerpt	Reference
Equal to the Father	"The Father is in Me, and I in the Father."	John 10:38
	". . . that all should honor the Son just as they honor the Father."	John 5:23 NKJV
	"He who sees Me sees Him who sent Me."	John 12:45 NKJV
Heir of God the Father	"In these last days [God] has spoken to us by his Son, whom he appointed heir of all things."	Heb. 1:2
	"All that belongs to the Father is mine."	John 16:15
	"All things have been committed to me by my Father."	Matt. 11:27
Omniscient	"Jesus knew what they were thinking."	Luke 5:22
	"Now we [apostles] can see that you [Jesus] know all things."	John 16:30
Omnipotent	". . . the Lord Jesus Christ, who, by the power that enables him to bring everything under his control . . ."	Phil. 3:20–21
Unchangeable	"Jesus Christ is the same yesterday and today and forever."	Heb. 13:8
Forgiving sin	"[Jesus] said to the paralytic, 'Son, your sins are forgiven.' "	Mark 2:5

Reymond.[7] Two historic church councils, Nicaea and Chalcedon, wrestled with this difficult theological issue and developed confessional documents to reaffirm the biblical Christian understanding of Jesus Christ's complete divinity and complete humanity.

Ali's commentary on Sura 19:34 remarks about this issue: "The disputations about the nature of Jesus Christ were vain, but also persistent and sanguinary. The modern Christian churches have thrown them into the background, but they would do well to abandon irrational dogmas altogether."

Far from being abandoned or thrown into the background, these historic documents and confessions are regularly referred to today by biblical Christian congregations to assist the church to stay true to the apostolic course of faith.

David Wells offers this succinct summary of the doctrine of incarnational Christology:

> If Yahweh is our sanctifier, is omnipresent, is our peace, is our righteousness, is our victory, and is our healer, then so is Christ all of these things (Ex. 31:13; Ps. 139:7–10; Judg. 6:24; Jer. 23:6; Ex. 17:8–16; Ex. 15:26; 1 Cor. 1:30; Col. 1:27; Eph. 2:14). If the gospel is God's, then that same gospel is also Christ's (1 Thess. 2:2, 6–9; Gal. 3:8; 1 Thess. 3:2; Gal. 1:7). If the church is God's, then that same church is also Christ's (Gal. 1:13; 1 Cor. 15:9; Rom. 16:16). God's Kingdom is Christ's (1 Thess. 2:12; Eph. 5:5); God's love is Christ's (Eph. 1:3–5; Rom. 8:35); God's Word is Christ's (Col. 1:25; 1 Thess. 2:13; 1 Thess. 1:8; 4:15); God's Spirit is Christ's (1 Thess. 4:8; Phil. 1:19); God's peace is Christ's (Gal. 5:22; Phil. 4:9; Col. 3:15; cf. Col. 1:2; Phil. 1:2; 4:7); God's "Day" of judgment is Christ's "Day" of judgment (Isa. 13:6; Phil. 1:6, 10; 2:16; 1 Cor. 1:8); God's salvation is Christ's salvation (Col. 1:13; 1 Thess. 1:10) and God's will is Christ's will (Eph. 1:11; 1 Thess. 4:3; Gal. 1:4; Eph. 5:17; cf. 1 Thess. 5:18).[8]

All the glorious attributes of Yahweh are possessed by Jesus Christ. He alone is able to fulfill all that Yahweh desires for his people and assume the threefold ministry of prophet, priest, and king (see table 13).

Jesus Christ is identified in many other roles within the Holy Scriptures: shepherd, head of the church, rabbi

TABLE 13   The ministry of Jesus Christ in the Holy Bible

Description	Excerpt	Reference
Prophet	"I will raise up for them a prophet like you from among their brothers."	Deut. 18:18
	"... My Elect One in whom My soul delights! I have put My Spirit upon Him."	Isa. 42:1 NKJV
	"The LORD has anointed me to preach good news to the poor."	Isa. 61:1; Luke 4:18
	"I know that His command is everlasting life."	John 12:50 NKJV
	"The one whom God has sent speaks the words of God."	John 3:34
	"... preaching the gospel of the kingdom ..."	Matt. 4:23 NKJV
	"The poor have the gospel preached to them."	Matt. 11:5 NKJV
	"Nor does anyone know the Father except the Son, and the one to whom the Son wills to reveal Him."	Matt. 11:27 NKJV
	"I have declared to them Your name."	John 17:26 NKJV
	"They were astonished at His teaching, for His word was with authority."	Luke 4:32 NKJV
	"False Christs and false prophets will appear and perform great signs and miracles to deceive even the elect—if that were possible. See, I have told you ahead of time."	Matt. 24:24–25
	"They will not leave in you [Jerusalem] one stone upon another."	Luke 19:44 NKJV
King	"Of the increase of His government and peace there will be no end, upon the throne of David and over his kingdom."	Isa. 9:7 NKJV
	"I will raise up to David a righteous Branch, a King who will reign wisely."	Jer. 23:5
	"Bethlehem Ephrathah ... out of you will come for me one who will be ruler over Israel."	Mic. 5:2
	"Where is the one who has been born king of the Jews?"	Matt. 2:2
	"He will be great and will be called the Son of the Most High. The Lord God will give him the throne of his father David."	Luke 1:32

TABLE 13   (continued)

Description	Excerpt	Reference
	"They took palm branches and went out to meet him, shouting. . . . 'Blessed is the King of Israel!' "	John 12:13
	"You are right in saying I am a king. In fact, for this reason I was born, and for this I came into the world, to testify to the truth. Everyone on the side of truth listens to me."	John 18:37
	"My kingdom is not of this world."	John 18:36
	"His kingdom will never end."	Luke 1:33
	"He has delivered us from the power of darkness and conveyed us into the kingdom of the Son of His love."	Col. 1:13 NKJV
	"We are receiving a kingdom that cannot be shaken."	Heb. 12:28
Messiah, mediator, priest	"He is the Mediator of the new covenant, by means of death, for the redemption of the transgressions under the first covenant, that those who are called may receive the promise of the eternal inheritance."	Heb. 9:15 NKJV
	"We have such a High Priest, who is seated at the right hand of the throne of the Majesty in the heavens."	Heb. 8:1 NKJV
	"For such a High Priest was fitting for us, who is holy, harmless, undefiled, separate from sinners."	Heb. 7:26 NKJV
	" 'Are you the Christ, the Son of the Blessed One?' 'I am,' said Jesus."	Mark 14:61–62
	"For there is one God and one mediator between God and men, the man Jesus Christ, who gave himself as a ransom for all men."	1 Tim. 2:5–6
	"He had to be made like His brethren, that He might be a merciful and faithful High Priest in things pertaining to God, to make propitiation for the sins of the people."	Heb. 2:17 NKJV
	"He is also Mediator of a better covenant, which was established on better promises."	Heb. 8:6 NKJV

TABLE 13   (*continued*)

Description	Excerpt	Reference
	"Consider the Apostle and High Priest of our confession, Christ Jesus, who was faithful to Him who appointed Him, as Moses also was faithful in all His house."	Heb. 3:1–2 NKJV
	"He always lives to intercede for them."	Heb. 7:25
	". . . till the Seed should come to whom the promise was made; and it was appointed through angels by the hand of a mediator."	Gal. 3:19 NKJV
	"The word of the oath, which came after the law, appoints the Son who has been perfected forever."	Heb. 7:28 NKJV
	"He has appeared to put away sin by the sacrifice of Himself."	Heb. 9:26 NKJV
	"We have a great high priest who has gone through the heavens, Jesus the Son of God."	Heb. 4:14
	"We do not have a high priest who is unable to sympathize with our weaknesses, but we have one who has been tempted in every way, just as we are—yet was without sin."	Heb. 4:15
	"He will be a priest on his throne."	Zech. 6:13

(preacher/teacher), healer, miracle-worker. We have concentrated here on just those three offices that were to find their fulfillment in the anticipated Messiah.

It is clear that a political leader was expected. Palestine had been oppressed by the occupation of the Roman Empire since 47 B.C. No prophet had arisen since Malachi. King Herod was a political puppet. The remnant of the early priesthood remained, but those ascending into this office were often corrupt and spiritually bankrupt. The desire was for a strong leader to take hold of the reins of power and overthrow the yoke of Caesar.

72

But Jesus Christ had a far greater mission—to preach and fulfill the gospel of Yahweh.

The gospel, as biblical Christians understand it, is the truly good news that the relationship between God and mankind is finally reestablished and that God calls human beings into full participation in that relationship. This is the kingdom of God to which people are called, and no earthly political kingdom can match it.

Yahweh's Everlasting Plan

All through history, men have honored and lauded great leaders and heroes in song, poetry, epic, and proclamation. Statues are erected and memorials are built. Around the world, legends abound regarding supermen who will return to establish kingdoms and rule with true equity and magnanimity. The one thing these stories have in common is the short-sightedness of their vision. They all focus only on this world.

Any human kingdom with the goal of a perfect perpetual earthly realm is destined to eventually fail. Any human kingdom that installs imperfect men in positions of ultimate authority will deteriorate over time. Any human kingdom that declares itself to be the expression and establishment of Divine Truth among mankind and roots itself in the temporary soil of this life will be unable to endure.

But a kingdom based on Divine Truth will have eternity at its core and infinity as its boundary. It is *not of this world.*

The ruler of God's kingdom must bridge the gap between the here and the hereafter, possessing the attributes of both divinity and humanity in their fullest sense. He can be no mere man, for he must rule forever. He can be no totally transcendent and remote god, for he must rule men. He must

73

be both God and man, for the soil into which this kingdom is planted is no less than the human heart.

This is exactly what Jesus Christ proclaimed. First-century Judaism did not understand it, and twenty-first-century Islam does not either.

"There's Something about That Name"

Jesus, Jesus, Jesus,
> There's just something about that Name
Master, Savior, Jesus,
> Like the fragrance after the rain . . .
Jesus, Jesus, Jesus,
> Let all heaven and earth proclaim.
Kings and kingdoms will all pass away,
> but there's something about that Name.
Jesus, the mere mention of His Name
> can calm the storm, heal the broken, and
> raise the dead . . .
At the Name of Jesus
> I've seen sin-hardened men melt, derelicts
> transformed,
> the lights of hope put back into the eyes of
> a hopeless child . . .
At the Name of Jesus
> hatred and bitterness turn to love and
> forgiveness
> arguments cease . . .
I've heard a mother softly breathe His Name
> at the bedside of a child delirious from fever
> and I've watched that little body grow quiet
> and the fevered brow cool . . .

74

I've sat beside a dying saint
    her body racked with pain
    who in those final fleeting seconds
    summoned her last ounce of having strength
    to whisper earth's sweetest Name,
Jesus, Jesus . . .
    Emperors have tried to destroy it
    Philosophers have tried to stamp it out
    Tyrants have tried to wash it from the face
    of the earth
    with the very blood of those who claimed it
    yet it still stands . . .
And there shall be that final day
    when every voice that has ever uttered
    a sound
    every voice of Adam's race
    shall raise in one great mighty chorus
    to proclaim the Name of Jesus . . .
For in that day every knee shall bow
    and every tongue shall confess
    that Jesus Christ is Lord.
So you see . . .
    it wasn't by mere chance
    that caused the angel one night long ago
    to say to a virgin maiden
His name shall be called
Jesus, Jesus, Jesus . . .
You know . . .
    there is something about that Name.[9]

4

THE NOBLE QUR'AN
AND THE HOLY BIBLE

Jews, Christians, and Muslims
all claim possession of inspired writings providing guidance
in doctrine and practice. The Hebrew Scriptures are the same
as the Old Testament of Christianity. Although the two faiths
divide the writings differently, the texts are identical. The
chronicle of the events of Jesus' life and ministry and the
development of his church are recounted in Christianity's
New Testament, so called because it represents the fulfillment of the promise of Yahweh for sinners' reconciliation
with him through the long-anticipated Messiah.

The Old and New Testaments are both included in their
entirety in the Holy Bible, which is the authoritative Scripture of Christians. The Old Testament has 39 books and the
New Testament 27 books. They were written by more than
40 different writers across a 1,500-year time span and are
assembled in roughly chronological order. Thus, it is possible to trace the self-revelation of Yahweh in a systematic
and orderly way through time from creation to the proph-
esied end of human history.

TEXTUAL VERIFICATION OF THE HOLY BIBLE

Scholars have repeatedly examined ancient manuscript copies of the Holy Bible and have confirmed its textual faithfulness and accuracy. Pursuing an in-depth discussion of biblical inerrancy is beyond the scope of this volume, but the reader is directed to the abundant scholarly publications dedicated to this subject, particularly Steven Mosood's *The Bible and the Qur'an: A Question of Integrity.* (This volume was first published in 2001 by OM publishing and reprinted in 2002 by Authentic Lifestyle, Cumbria, UK). No other ancient literature or manuscript has endured the intense scrutiny and verification that the Holy Bible has undergone. Nor does any other ancient document have as many surviving manuscripts and copies.

THE NOBLE QUR'AN

The Noble Qur'an is considered by Muslims to be "the actual Word of God revealed through the archangel Gabriel to the Prophet of Islam during the twenty-three year period of his prophetic mission. It was revealed in the Arabic language as a sonoral revelation which the Prophet repeated to his companions."[1] The word *Qur'an* can be translated "cry" or "recite." Muhammad heard this command to orally repeat what he was told.

According to translator Marmaduke Pickthall, the Noble Qur'an is described as "that inimitable symphony the very sounds of which move men to tears and ecstasy."[2] It was meant to be recited and heard. The early suras particularly "are characterized by a hymnic quality, condensed and powerful imagery, and a sweeping lyricism."[3]

Muslim children typically begin with the shorter, earlier suras when taught to chant the Noble Qur'an in Arabic, and these are the portions most often memorized and recited. In written texts of the Noble Qur'an, however, the 114 suras are assembled according to length, with the longest passages presented first. Because it is not possible to decisively pinpoint the chronological order of the suras, it is more difficult to interpret the historical development of Islamic thought. Most Islamic scholars believe they are able to determine which portions were recited during Muhammad's exile in Medina and which ones came to him after his return to Mecca.

Most English translations of the Noble Qur'an are difficult for Western readers to follow. It is not a book that one can sit and read chapter by chapter, in logical progression. The Noble Qur'an "shifts thematic registers: from mystical passages to sacred history, from law to the struggles of Muhammad and his followers with little or no warning. Many of its chapters mix themes that sometimes begin in mid-topic."[4]

In Islamic countries, life is bathed with public broadcasts of Qur'anic recitation. The fragmented sections are eventually rearranged into cogent narratives in the minds of listeners through continual exposure. Recordings of the most popular Qur'anic reciters are available in stores throughout the Muslim world.

The Qur'an is the central sacred reality of Islam. The sound of the Qur'an is the first and last sound that a Muslim hears in this life. Essentially a religion of the book, Islam sees all authentic religions as being associated with a scripture. That is why Muslims call Christians and Jews the "people of the Book."[5]

HOW ISLAM VIEWS THE HOLY BIBLE

The Noble Qur'an exhorts readers to believe in previous revelation (Sura 2:136; 4:163) and to obtain counsel from "those who have been reading the Book from before you" (Sura 10:94). The previous revelation is the Holy Bible, and those who have been reading it are the Jews and Christians. Yet the Holy Bible is not included within the covers of any edition of the Noble Qur'an. Why is this?

Muslims maintain that the previous Scriptures were corrupted and can no longer be trusted. The footnote for Sura 2:135 in Ali's translation of the Noble Qur'an declares that the creed of Islam includes belief in "the message delivered by other Teachers in the past." Ali delineates these teachers into three groups: Abraham, Isma'il, Isaac, Jacob, and the Tribes, with Abraham being given a Book; Moses; and Jesus, "who each left a scripture; these Scriptures are still extant, *though not in their pristine form*" (italics ours); and other scriptures not specifically mentioned in the Noble Qur'an. Ali asserts that the essential message of all these revelations is consistent with Islam. His commentary is based on accepted Islamic theology.

Since the Noble Qur'an is considered to be the final word of Allah to man, it is also considered to be complete. For Muslims, therefore, the Holy Bible provides no further spiritual insight.

These two factors—doubt about its reliability and assertions of its irrelevancy—make the Holy Bible anathema to Muslims.

SEARCHING THE SCRIPTURES

It must be boldly but respectfully stated that no extant evidence supports any of Islam's disparaging statements about the Holy Bible's reliability. Generally, religions that cast suspicion on the authenticity of the Holy Bible do so to prevent followers from careful, thoughtful study of Scripture to determine the validity of the "new revelation." Removing the support of family, friends, and sacred writings, or causing them to be regarded with suspicion, gives the new religion a free pass into the soul of the convert.

If Islam truly supports the contention that it "places the gaining of knowledge as the highest religious activity, one that is most pleasing in God's eyes,"[6] then it should encourage the study of all sacred writings, especially the contemporary texts of the "previous Scriptures." If it is truly all "of one piece" with Truth, the "old" should verify the "new."

Roy Gustafson, internationally known authority on prophecy and Bible lands, sums up this principle:

The New Testament is contained in the Old Testament.
The Old Testament is explained in the New Testament.

The New Testament is concealed in the Old Testament.
The Old Testament is revealed in the New Testament.

The Old Testament anticipates the New Testament.
The New Testament authenticates the Old Testament.

In the Old Testament the New Testament lies hidden.
In the New Testament the Old Testament lies open.

The Old Testament foreshadows the New Testament.
The New Testament fulfills the Old Testament.

In the Old Testament they were always seeking.
In the New Testament they found.

The Old Testament predicts a Person.
The New Testament presents that Person.

And the Person is the Lord Jesus Christ—who fully
validated the Old Testament.

The Pentateuch (the first five books of the Bible)
presents the Figures of Christ.

The Psalms present the Feelings of Christ.
The Prophets present the Foretellings of Christ.

The Gospels present the Facts of Christ.
The Epistles present the Fruits of Christ.[7]

The biblical Triune God is fully capable of preserving and
maintaining the integrity of his self-revelatory record
throughout time. He desires men to use it as a guide and
standard for instruction.

Searching the Scriptures was a common practice among
early Christian believers. Acts 17:11 reports that "the Bere-
ans were of more noble character than the Thessalonians, for
they received the message with great eagerness and *examined
the Scriptures every day* to see if what Paul said was true"
(italics ours). Scriptural scholarship was encouraged by the
apostles and became the habit of the emerging Christian community. The Holy Scriptures were so important to Paul that
he specifically asked Timothy to bring them to him: "When
you come, bring the cloak that I left . . . and my scrolls, especially the parchments" (2 Tim. 4:13). In all fairness, the early
followers of Muhammad, even Muhammad himself, did not

have access to translated Arabic Scriptures in the seventh century A.D. But today's Muslims cannot use the same excuse.

Since we have been studying the truth about Truth, as defined in chapter 1, let's look more closely at the way in which the word *truth* is used in each document (see tables 14 and 15).

Although these are just sample passages from each text, a broader discussion of Truth is given in the Holy Bible than in the Noble Qur'an. In the Holy Bible, the word *truth* is applied in a variety of ways: as a personal characteristic and possession of Yahweh; as a desired characteristic of his people and his church; as a description of his book (the Holy Bible), the gospel, and his city (Jerusalem); as a guide for

TABLE 14   "Truth" in the Noble Qur'an

Excerpt	Sura
"Such is Allah, your real Cherisher and Sustainer: apart from Truth, what (remains) but error?"	10:32
"And say: 'Truth has (now) arrived, and Falsehood perished.' "	17:81
"Nay, We hurl the Truth against falsehood, and it knocks out its brain."	21:18
"Or do they say, 'he is possessed?' Nay, he has brought them the Truth, but most of them hate the Truth."	23:70–71
"We have sent them the Truth: but they indeed practice Falsehood!"	23:90
"Or do they say, 'He has forged it?' Nay, it is the Truth from your Lord, that you may admonish a people."	32:3
"Say: 'Verily my Lord casts the (mantle of) Truth (over His servants).' "	34:48
"That which We have revealed to you of the Book is the Truth, confirming what was (revealed) before it."	35:31
". . . until it becomes manifest to them that this is the Truth."	41:53
"Ah woe, that Day, to the Rejecters of Truth!"	77:15
"Those who reject (Truth), among the People of the Book . . . will be in hell-fire."	98:6

TABLE 15   Truth in the Holy Bible

Excerpt	Reference
"Into your hands I commit my spirit; redeem me, O LORD, the God of truth."	Ps. 31:5
"Surely you desire truth in the inner parts; you teach me wisdom."	Ps. 51:6
"But first I will tell you what is written in the Book of Truth."	Dan. 10:21
"Then Jerusalem will be called the City of Truth."	Zech. 8:3
"We know you [Jesus] are a man of integrity and that you teach the way of God in accordance with the truth."	Matt. 22:16
"For the law was given through Moses; grace and truth came through Jesus Christ."	John 1:17
"Christ has become a servant of the Jews on behalf of God's truth, to confirm the promises made to the patriarchs so that the Gentiles may glorify God for his mercy, as it is written . . ."	Rom. 15:8–9
"Love does not delight in evil but rejoices with the truth."	1 Cor. 13:6
"And you also were included in Christ when you heard the word of truth, the gospel of your salvation."	Eph. 1:13
". . . God's household, which is the church of the living God, the pillar and foundation of the truth."	1 Tim. 3:15

teaching, coupled with grace in the Person of Jesus Christ; and as a partner to love and joy.

The words for *truth* in Hebrew and Greek, languages very rich in meaning, are sometimes translated into English as "faithfulness," "support," "firmness," and "steadfastness," and these terms are often used in reference to Yahweh. They emphasize that he is dependable, consistent, and trustworthy— the characteristics of Divine Truth.

In the Qur'anic verses, the word *Truth* is most frequently used for the message that Muhammad recited. Often it is sharply contrasted with falsehood in the same sentence or sura.

MUHAMMAD'S DEFENSE

Note particularly the passage from Sura 23:70. This was directed to those who compared Muhammad's unusual visionary behaviors to demonic possession (see chap. 2). Many of Muhammad's contemporaries raised this objection to his claim to spiritual authority. Muhammad was continually forced to defend himself, reiterating that his message was that of "truth" and admonishing the people to believe in him.

Significantly, *at no time* does Muhammad identify *himself* with Truth, as Jesus Christ did. Muhammad did not claim deity, nor did he assert personal sinlessness, although the latter has been attributed to him in Islamic theology.

Positive and descriptive qualities reinforcing, honoring, and enriching the concept of Truth are abundant in the Holy Bible. Very few of these are present in Muhammad's recitation. If we attempt to derive deep insight into the nature of Truth from the Noble Qur'an, we come away unsatisfied.

NON-TRUTH

A comparison of other biblical and Qur'anic texts— those using terms such as *falsehood, deception,* and *lying* reveals how differently they handle the concept of non-Truth (see tables 16 and 17).

Qur'anic passages primarily refer to falsehood as characteristic of the remarks of those who disbelieve the Qur'anic message or reject Muhammad. Numerous verses admonish unbelievers with similar terminology. Many of these verses are meant to be repeated verbatim in response to challenges to the faith and are preceded by the imperative "say."

The Qur'anic assertion in Sura 4:142, that Allah "overreaches" man, is interesting. This is alternatively translated

TABLE 16 Sample "non-Truth" passages in the Noble Qur'an

Excerpt	Sura
"The Hypocrites—they think they are over-reaching Allah, but He will over-reach them."	4:142
"They uttered against Mary a grave false charge; That they said (in boast), 'We killed Christ Jesus the son of Mary, the Messenger of Allah';—but they did not kill him, nor crucified him."	4:156–57
"It is those who do not believe in the Signs of Allah, that forge falsehood; it is they who lie!"	16:105
"(Who) is better?—Allah or the false gods they associate (with Him)?"	27:59
"Certain it is that either we or you are on right guidance or in manifest error!"	34:24
"Woe to each sinful dealer in Falsehoods: He hears the Signs of Allah rehearsed to him, yet is obstinate and lofty."	45:7–8
"The unbelievers say, of the Truth when it comes to them: 'This is evident sorcery!' "	46:7
"Woe to the falsehood-mongers,—those who (flounder) Heedless in a flood of confusion."	51:10–11
"(Their allies deceived them), like the Evil One, when he says to man, 'Deny Allah.' "	59:16
"Who does greater wrong than one who invents falsehood against Allah . . . ?"	61:7
"I warn you of a Fire blazing fiercely; None shall reach it but those most unfortunate ones Who give the lie to Truth and turn their backs."	92:14–16
"Woe to every (kind of) scandal-monger and backbiter."	104:1

as "deceives," "connives," "plots," or "plans." If Allah is able to deceive, then he must not be fully truthful. If he is not fully truthful, then he is not trustworthy. How, then, do we know when to believe him?

TRUSTWORTHINESS OF YAHWEH

The Holy Bible asserts that "it is impossible for God to lie" (Heb. 6:18) and, referring to the Messiah, that "nor was any deceit in his mouth" (Isa. 53:9). Lies and deceit are in direct opposition to Divine Truth. It would be contrary to the inherent nature of Yahweh to engage in them. This also means that Yahweh will not alter his message, nor will he fail to fulfill his promises.

The biblical Triune God does not assert one thing at one time, then assert the opposite at another time; nor does he alter his revelation to suit man. That would be inconsistent and would violate the nature of Divine Truth. Yahweh always acts in accordance with his own perfect nature.

The biblical passages also give us greater insight into the various forms in which non-Truth can appear: false testimony, false dreams, false apostles, false humility, and false

TABLE 17   Sample "non-Truth" passages in the Holy Bible

Excerpt	Reference
"You shall not give false testimony against your neighbor."	Ex. 20:16
"Keep falsehood and lies far from me; give me neither poverty nor riches."	Prov. 30:8
". . . though he had done no violence, nor was any deceit in his mouth."	Isa. 53:9
" 'Indeed, I am against those who prophesy false dreams,' declares the LORD. 'They tell them and lead my people astray with their reckless lies, yet I did not send or appoint them.' "	Jer. 23:32
". . . and many false prophets will appear and deceive many people."	Matt. 24:11
"For from within, out of men's hearts, come evil thoughts, sexual immorality, theft, murder, adultery, greed, malice, deceit, lewdness, envy, slander, arrogance, and folly."	Mark 7:21–22
"For such men are false apostles, deceitful workmen, masquerading as apostles of Christ."	2 Cor. 11:13
"Such regulations indeed have an appearance of wisdom, with their self-imposed worship, their false humility, and their harsh treatment of the body, but they lack any value."	Col. 2:23
"If anyone teaches false doctrines and does not agree to the sound instruction of our Lord Jesus Christ and to godly teaching, he is conceited and understands nothing."	1 Tim. 6:3
"It is impossible for God to lie."	Heb. 6:18

doctrines. The Bible is full of warnings not to accept strange teachings. Biblical believers are advised to cling to the Truth and not be taken in by deceivers who claim to have some sort of special revelation from any divine being if that message differs from what they have been taught. Paul warned believers that even if an angel should come preaching a different message, it should be rejected (Gal. 1:8–9).

QUICK CONVERSIONS

By contrast, the Noble Qur'an continually admonishes people, especially those with previous scriptural teaching, not to reject its message. The new and strange teaching of Muhammad is to be embraced without delay. Pressure to hastily receive any revelation is not within the biblical pattern. Yet the Noble Qur'an makes the appeal for quick conversion regularly, by the command of Allah.

One contemporary Muslim appeal to atheists is particularly interesting. In the online article entitled "Comparative Religions" at www.islaminfo.com, we read that

the Atheist can simply submit in Islam although he still has doubt. Rather than argue about what he doubts he should first *get on the safe side* and then investigate further. The reasonable thing, then, is for the Atheist to *accept Islam right away*. If he will not take this reasonable position, then why should you argue with an unreasonable person? Just remind him that even if Islam is wrong you are still safe. But if Islam is right he is in deep trouble.[8]

It is not reasonable to rush into association with any religion without careful thought, investigation, and prayer. Is the impulsive recitation of the shahada ("There is no god but Allah and Muhammad is the Prophet of Allah"), motivated only by the desire to "get on the safe side," a valid confession of faith? Will that put a person in right standing with Allah? What does "being on the safe side" really mean, anyway, since Allah decides individual eternal destinies solely on the basis of his own whim? And finally, after the person "submits," is he then given the freedom and encouragement to investigate further? Let's do that here. Since both texts affirm divine inspiration, it is interesting to look at what each one asserts about *itself* (see tables 18 and 19).

ASSEMBLY OF THE NOBLE QUR'AN

The passages from the Noble Qur'an reveal several intriguing characteristics about the writings. For instance, it is in sections, in "your own tongue" (Arabic), and inscribed on an "imperishable tablet."

Some background on the assembly of the Noble Qur'an is necessary here. Although the publication *Islam: A Global Civilization* states that "under the direction of the Prophet, the verses and chapters were organized in the order known to Muslims to this day,"[9] Islamic scholars confirm that the Noble Qur'an was not codified within Muhammad's lifetime. It was collated after his death from documentation of his sayings made on such items as bone fragments, leaves, and hides, and augmented by the memories of close associates. Traditions vary regarding who actually began and finalized the formal compilation. Caliph Uthman (who was eventually assassinated by dissenting Muslims), third "rightly guided caliph" after the death of Muhammad, is generally given the credit. One of the motivating factors for assembling the sayings in a

89

TABLE 18 Self-assertions in the Noble Qur'an

Assertion	Sura
It is the book of Moses and Jesus.	2:87
Its verses are fundamental and allegorical.	3:7
It gives guidance.	3:73
It is an inspired message.	4:82; 6:19
Allah is witness; it shows Allah's revelation.	6:19, 92; 27:6
It is a book of Wisdom.	10:1; 31:2; 36:2
It is not to be made into shreds.	15:91
It shows the purpose of revelation.	16:64–65
It is given through the Holy Spirit.	16:102–3
It is good news and warning.	17:9–10
It offers healing and mercy; is easy.	17:82; 19:97; 44:58; 54:17
It explains similitudes.	17:89; 18:54
It is revealed in stages.	17:106; 25:32
It contains no crookedness.	18:1–2
It instructs mankind, is taught by Allah	18:2–4; 19:97; 20:2–7; 39:41; 55:1–2
It solves Israel's controversies.	27:76
It carries its own evidence.	29:47–49
It is Truth from Allah.	32:3; 35:31
It is to be used for admonishing.	50:45
It is to be received with humility.	59:21
It is a Message to all the Worlds.	81:26–29
Unbelievers reject it.	84:20–25
It is a Tablet preserved in heaven.	85:21–22
It is a Word that distinguishes Good from Evil.	86:11–14
It is to be proclaimed.	96:1

book was that many followers possessing firsthand knowledge of Muhammad's recitations were dying in battle and the passages they had memorized were being lost.

The Noble Qur'an is indeed in sections, which have been given names to distinguish them from each other. There is no doubt that Muhammad recited them at different times and, therefore, as a "gradual revelation."

Described as being revealed "in your own tongue," the Noble Qur'an's use of Arabic is especially interesting. Reading Sura 19, one would get the impression that Arabic was the vernacular of the day. But this is not the case. Arabian tribes in the seventh century A.D. spoke a wide variety of dialects. Even today, many Muslims learn to recite the Noble Qur'an in Arabic as prescribed by Islamic tradition, but do not understand a word of it. The Arabic language has assumed the aura of a "holy language" within Islam. In fact, any translation of the Noble Qur'an into another language is not regarded as authoritative, but only as an interpretation of the text.

TABLE 19   Self-assertions in the Holy Bible

Excerpt	Reference
"All Scripture is God-breathed and is useful for teaching, rebuking, correcting and training in righteousness."	2 Tim. 3:16
". . . the word planted in you."	James 1:21
". . . the Book of Truth."	Dan. 10:21
". . . the law of the LORD."	Ps. 1:2
". . . the scroll of the LORD."	Isa. 34:16
". . . the gospel he promised beforehand."	Rom. 1:2
". . . the word of the prophets made more certain."	2 Peter 1:19
". . . able to make you wise . . ."	2 Tim. 3:15
"These are the Scriptures that testify about me [Jesus Christ]."	John 5:39
". . . written to teach us."	Rom. 15:4
". . . preserves my life; true . . . eternal; perfect, precious . . ."	Pss. 119:50, 160; 19:7, 10
". . . birth through the word of truth."	James 1:18
". . . written that you may believe."	John 20:31
". . . [to be read] all the days of his life."	Deut. 17:19
"Man does not live on bread alone, but on every word that comes from the mouth of God."	Matt. 4:4
"There I find delight."	Ps. 119:35

TRANSLATION OF THE HOLY BIBLE

Translation of the Bible into the vernacular of all people groups has always been considered an essential part of the propagation of the divine message. Historically, this began very early.

The quotations of Old Testament Scripture used in writing the New Testament were taken from the very popular first-century Greek version of the Hebrew Scriptures, the Septuagint, named for the 70 Jewish scholars of Alexandria, Egypt, who collaborated on its translation in the third and second centuries B.C. Both the Old and New Testaments have subsequently been translated into all the major languages on earth. Translation work is ongoing among smaller populations with unique or unwritten languages. Entire ministries have devoted themselves to this single task.

Resources on the process of biblical translation can be found in any Christian bookstore, or in the prefaces of most editions of the Holy Bible, especially study Bibles used for teaching and exegesis.

TRANSCENDENTAL REVELATION

Muslims believe that the Noble Qur'an is a "Tablet preserved" physically in heaven by Allah and kept safe from any human corruption. It is said to have been written in Arabic eternally and guarded by Allah. This concept has no precedent in biblical tradition. Even the Ten Commandments delivered to Moses on Mount Sinai, believed to be "inscribed by the hand of God," were not described as having been kept in physical form in any other place before being delivered to Moses.

92

The Islamic concept of the translation of heavenly documents is called "transcendental revelation," described as the "vertical movement of transcendent information 'from above' down to the level of man."[10] Muslims believe that only this type of transmission makes a text divinely inspired.

HISTORICAL-INSPIRATIONAL REVELATION

The historical-inspirational form of revelation is attested to in the Holy Bible. Biblical Christians believe that although God is above and beyond history and, indeed, beyond time itself, he shows himself and his sovereignty over all creation by his historical activity within that creation. The Holy Bible, with Yahweh as its author, is given to us through the writings of chosen men under the inspiration of the Holy Spirit, within their historical-cultural context. This gives the text authenticity and strength.

On the other hand, the Noble Qur'an, with Allah as its author, was given privately to Muhammad in ecstatic recitations during spiritual visitations while he was enduring unusual physiological symptoms. Muhammad had no witnesses to verify that Allah gave him the Noble Qur'an through the angel Gabriel.

The two methods cannot be reconciled.

A SUMMARY OF THE NOBLE QUR'AN

So when we take a comprehensive look at the Noble Qur'an, we conclude the following:

• The Noble Qur'an is a book of law.

- The Noble Qur'an is about Allah as master and humankind as his slaves.
- The Noble Qur'an is about submission to Allah— no questions asked.
- The Noble Qur'an teaches a religious, social, and political system.
- The Noble Qur'an is about the "seal of the prophets," who is Muhammad, and his recitation, which is the Noble Qur'an itself.

Its primary focus is to elicit faith in Muhammad's sayings, deliver a law to the Arabic people for the regulation of life and worship, and assert the absolute sovereignty of the singular god, Allah.

- The Noble Qur'an is not a book about biblical salvation.
- The Noble Qur'an is not about the love of God for sinners.
- The Noble Qur'an is not about eternal life in Christ Jesus.
- The Noble Qur'an is not about Christ's victory at his second coming.
- The Noble Qur'an is not about knowing God and having a personal relationship with him.

The Noble Qur'an is not intended to be used by the Holy Spirit to regenerate the heart of man, give him joy or hope, or produce in him true obedience. Although it mentions Jesus Christ as the Messiah, it does not confirm the biblical testimony of him as the Son of the living God. The messianic concepts of salvation through him, faith in him, and assurance of eternal life through and with him are entirely absent.

A SUMMARY OF THE HOLY BIBLE

Careful consideration of the Holy Bible reveals the following:

- The Holy Bible is a book about salvation through Jesus Christ, who saves his people from their sin.
- The Holy Bible is about Yahweh, who made himself known through his Son, Jesus Christ.
- The Holy Bible foreshadows the second coming of Christ Jesus, and anticipates it with joy.
- The Holy Bible is about knowing Yahweh personally.
- The Holy Bible is about Yahweh's love for the sinful human race.
- The Holy Bible is about the eternal life found only in Jesus Christ.

THE ESSENTIAL QUESTION

If we refer back to the assertion made by the Saudi Arabian publication *Islam: A Global Civilization*, the following question begs an answer: In what way does Qur'anic Islam support and continue the truths found in biblical theology, as it claims? For there is no doubt, even after the limited overview presented here, that the Noble Qur'an and the Holy Bible are two very different texts, delivering two very different central messages.

"A Prayer for the Muslim World"
(CONTINUED)

... Strengthen converts,
restore backsliders,
and give all those
who labor among Muslims
the tenderness of Christ,
so that bruised reeds
may become pillars
of his church,
and smoking flaxwicks
burning and shining lights.
Make bare thine arm,
O God,
and show thy power.
All our expectation
is from thee ...

5

THE GODHEAD IN
QUR'ANIC AND BIBLICAL
THOUGHT

One God. Both Muslims and Christians begin their religious journeys with this assertion. The theological term for this concept is *monotheism*. It asserts that the Divine Being to whom mankind should direct its worship and devotion is one entity. He alone is the supreme sovereign over all creation and is omnipotent, omniscient, and omnipresent.

Today, many people are under the impression that all monotheistic religions direct their worship to the same god. After all, they all call this deity "God," in one language or another, don't they? A "god" is a "God" is a "god," isn't it? Or, more directly, Allah is Yahweh is "the Force." It's all the same thing, right?

Wrong. Similarity of names does not make objects identical or even related. Language serves only to "tag" our experiences. To truly communicate, words must transmit meaning as well. Meaning requires depth of thought. Thinking is difficult. Consequently, many contemporary religious organizations have adopted a warm, fuzzy "god," whose only definable characteristics are that he is completely nonjudgmental and totally benevolent. This god makes no demands and offers no challenges. He has no real power, no genuine relevance in this life. He is made of putty, pressed and molded to serve the emotional needs of believers. Faith in him is a lazy faith—a feel-good philosophy for the common man.

Man exchanges omnipotence for impotence, omniscience for indulgence, and sacrificial love for sentimentality. This is a poor exchange, indeed!

Neither Qur'anic Muslims nor biblical Christians recognize deity in such a concept. Both Allah and Yahweh have very distinct and identifiable characteristics that set them in sharp relief against such nebulous nonsense. This is the important question to be asked: Are the characteristics of Allah and Yahweh so similar that they can rightly be said to represent the same deity?

THE ISLAMIC ALLAH

Examining the nature of Allah is complicated, since "the Muslim view implies that to all intents and purposes God is unknowable . . . Muslims will often claim to have a knowledge of God, but they mean by that a knowledge of truth *about* God, not the knowledge of God as a person."[1] Allah does not have an identifiable personality, nor does he reveal anything about himself to man. In Islamic thought, the very idea is sacrilegious. Man can know only Allah's will, nothing more.

One can know many things about other beings (human or divine) and yet remain a total stranger to those beings. Other beings can choose to withhold information about themselves and prevent intimate friendship from developing. True knowledge and understanding of each other implies that both beings desire to know and be known, to share themselves with each other, to spend time together and have common experiences. Both must be willing for fellowship and intimacy to occur.

The god Allah does not seek fellowship with man. Allah's will is that man submit to him, not sup with him.

On the other hand, we have the Christian God, Yahweh, who spent time in the Garden of Eden and sought out Adam and Eve (Gen. 3:8–9). Here is a God who takes the first step to form a relationship with man. Here is a God who not only initiated time and human history, but breaks into it regularly and undeniably in order to make himself known. Here is a God who gave his own Son to bridge the gap between heaven and earth.

Tables 20 and 21 show what the sacred texts teach about the defining characteristics of deity. In these tables we have deliberately selected passages that show superficial similarities between Allah and Yahweh with regard to selected characteristics. But looks can be deceiving. In table 22, we see passages showing sharp contrast between the two texts in several attributes.

THE RADICAL UNITY OF ALLAH

While the Holy Bible proclaims, "Hear, O Israel: The LORD our God, the LORD is one" (Deut. 6:4; cf. Mark 12:29), Islam embraces what may be called the "radical unity" of Allah. It considers itself the "religion of Oneness." Allah is so absolutely singular, so totally separate, that he cannot even be imagined. He has no body, no spirit. He needs noth-

TABLE 20   Characteristics of deity in the Noble Qur'an

Attribute	Excerpt	Sura
One	". . . no god but He."	28:88
Creator	"He gave order and perfection to the seven firmaments."	2:29
Sovereign	"He is the Most High, the Supreme in Glory."	2:255
Merciful, forgiving	"Allah forgives all sins."	39:53
Omnipotent	"Allah hath power over all things."	2:284
Incomparable	"There is nothing like unto Him."	42:11
Omniscient	"Allah knows it all."	3:29
Eternal	"Allah, the Eternal"	112:2
Invisible	"No vision can grasp Him, but His grasp is over all vision."	6:103
Wise	"For Allah hath full knowledge."	4:35
Living	". . . the Living, the Self-subsisting, Eternal."	2:255
Loving	". . . full of mercy and loving-kindness."	11:90
Avenging	"Allah is strict in punishment."	59:7

ing, wants nothing, feels nothing, possesses nothing. "For some Islamic theologians, to give the deity separate attributes threatens the unity of God."[2] Consequently, Allah is most often described in terms of what he is *not*. Allah is defined by a series of negations. "The great Imams are agreed regarding the danger and impiety of studying or discussing the nature of the being of God."[3] Farid Esack writes in his book *On Being a Muslim* that "all our doctrinal formulations and perceptions of Allah are just those; as for Allah, He is the eternally 'greater.' "[4] Al-Ghazali, famous Muslim scholastic, has "un-described" Allah this way:

Allah is not a body endued with form nor a substance circumscribed with limits or determined by measure. Neither does He resemble bodies, as they are capable of being measured or divided. Neither is He a substance, nor do substances exist in Him; neither is He

TABLE 21 Characteristics of deity in the Holy Bible

Attribute	Excerpt	Reference
One	"The LORD is one!"	Deut. 6:4
Creator	"God created the heavens and the earth."	Gen. 1:1
Sovereign	"My [Yahweh's] purpose will stand."	Isa. 46:10
Merciful, forgiving	"As a father has compassion . . . so the LORD has compassion."	Ps. 103:13
Omnipotent	"Nothing is too hard for you."	Jer. 32:17, 27
Incomparable	"There is no one like you, and there is no God but you."	2 Sam. 7:22
Omniscient	"God . . . knows everything."	1 John 3:20
Eternal	"the King eternal"	1 Tim. 1:17
Invisible	"No one has ever seen God."	John 1:18
Wise	". . . God who alone is wise . . ."	1 Tim. 1:17 NKJV
Living	"The LORD is the true God . . . the living God."	Jer. 10:10
Loving	"God is love."	1 John 4:8, 16
Avenging	"It is mine [Yahweh's] to avenge."	Deut. 32:35

an accident [quality], nor do accidents exist in Him. Neither is He like to anything that exists; neither is anything like Him. His nearness is not like the nearness of bodies nor is His essence like the essence of bodies. Neither does He exist in anything nor does anything exist in Him.[5]

How can we grasp this idea of God? This is an honest inquiry into the heart of Islam. How can a relationship be pursued with a being who, for all intents and purposes, cannot and will not be known? Writes Reformed theologian and pastor Dr. James Boice:

There are two ways to define something, and both are necessary. One way is by telling what the object in

TABLE 22 Contrasts in characteristics of deity

Attribute	Qur'anic excerpt	Sura	Biblical excerpt	Reference
One	"They do blaspheme who say: Allah is one of three."	5:72–73	"... baptizing them in the name of the Father and of the Son and of the Holy Spirit."	Matt. 28:19–20
Merciful, forgiving	"The reward is forgiveness from their Lord."	57:21	"If we confess our sins, he is faithful and just and will forgive us."	1 John 1:9
Loving	"Allah's object also is ... to deprive of blessing those that resist Faith.... Allah loves those who act aright."	3:141, 76	"God demonstrates his own love for us in this: While we were still sinners, Christ died for us."	Rom. 5:8
Avenging	"The curse of Allah is on the wrong-doers."	6:160	"He does not treat us as our sins deserve."	Ps. 103:9–10

question *is*. The other way is by telling what it is *not*. Both are important because if you cannot say what it is not, then the object may very well be everything and consequently nothing. On the other hand, it is also necessary to say what the object is, because the negatives at best merely narrow down the possibilities.[6]

Within Islam, the possibilities are narrow indeed. Insistence on Allah's total transcendence makes him not only *im*personal, but also as *un*personal as a being can get. "In Islam, it is not possible to say that humanity is made in God's image, because there would then be something of God beside Himself."[7] A god such as Allah, with no human point of reference in either concept or thought, is like a word without an idea. It is essentially meaningless. By limiting the characterization of Allah to primarily that which he is not, Muslims effectively nullify his practical existence for mankind.

Muslims are correct in saying that one cannot know Allah. Humanly speaking, there is literally nothing to know.

THE COMPLEX UNITY OF THE BIBLICAL TRINITY

A categorical defense of God's unity at the expense of any sense of personality within the divine nature invariably leads into conflict with Christian doctrine. Christians should ask Muslims to explain if the oneness of God must necessarily be defined as a mathematical unity or if it could also be expressed as a complex unity.[8]

What, exactly, is a "complex unity"? We would define it as *a single entity with multiple manifestations that are of the same essence.* Each manifestation fully represents the whole, and the whole fully resides in each manifestation.

In the Trinity all the attributes of the one divine Being are possessed by and reflected in each Person. God's three Persons and his abundant attributes eternally coexist and cohere in the singular essence of the eternal Godhead.

Muslim scholars find this incomprehensible: "If those attributes are eternal, then there is a diversity of eternal, separate powers."[9] When biblical Christians quote "God is love" from 1 John 4:8, or Jesus' statement "I and the Father are one" in John 10:30, the passages bring great comfort to them, but give Muslims great discomfort. In Islam, this view makes Christians guilty of "shirk"—associating partners with God.

Biblical Christians maintain that the unity of Yahweh is not limited to a numerical oneness, nor is he denigrated or divided by his association with differentiated characteristics. His nature is expanded by his divine personality in all its glorious complexity.

Misinformation about this issue abounds in the Muslim community. Sura 5:73 uses the inaccurate phrase "one of three," demonstrating Muhammad's incomplete understanding of Christian doctrine. Even today, the doctrine of the tri-unity of the Godhead is referred to as "a vague and mysterious doctrine that was formulated during the fourth century."[10] The writer adds, "One person, God the Father + one person, God the Son + one person, God the Holy Ghost = one person, God the What? Is this English or is this gibberish?"[11] The mistake in that equation is that the biblical Triune God is not a composite of three Persons who come together to form one Person. By stating it in this manner, the author reveals that he is thinking in purely human terms, not in the language of the divine.

The article continues:

The God of the Christians was now seen as having three essences, or natures, in the form of the Father, the Son, and the Holy Spirit.

Trinity designates God as being three separate entities.[12]

Both of these statements are in error. Yahweh is not three entities or three essences. *Yahweh is one entity, and his essence is one.* The divine nature is *unique,* even while encompassing three equally divine persons.

These sources are not cited in order to engage in fruitless debate or argument. We are not attacking or trying to belittle the author in any way. But biblical Christians are just as concerned about the truthful presentation of our beliefs as Muslims are about the presentation of their own. Honest questioning is welcomed, but misrepresentation is not.

Though all of this may seem unnecessarily metaphysical, it has important practical applications. Biblical Christianity worships the "God who is there," as Francis Schaeffer asserted. This God can be imagined in all his complexity and glory, in a limited and childlike way, by his people.

How can one imagine a deity who exists as a complex unity? This has always presented a quandary for theologians. Legend has it that Ireland's St. Patrick attempted to give tri-unity visual form by using the crude analogy of the three-leaved shamrock. Others have tried offering a parallel with the human experience of multiple roles: a man can be a son, a husband, and a father. The full self is present and applied to each role, but no role is objectively greater or less than the others, and all roles are represented by one being. But these are awkward comparisons at best.

Fortunately for us, Yahweh invites inquiry and understands man's flawed, yet sincere, attempts to find a suitable description for him. He helps us along by choosing to present himself to us in images and ideas that we can appreciate. His complex unity is fully expressed in his divine Persons: the Father, the Son, and the Holy Spirit. These Persons coexist eternally in loving relationship with one another and share all the characteristics of Divine Truth. This is the biblical Christian understanding of the Triune God.

Now we come to the crux of the matter. Since the three Persons of the Triune God stand in relationship, the relational pattern of man to man and man to God is established. "God cannot be solitary if He is loving. This idea of God in communion with humanity brings with it a view which is beyond monism, because God Himself exists in interrelationship."[13] Biblical Christianity emphatically affirms that reverent familiarity with the personality of Yahweh, through his Son and sanctified by his Spirit, is in fact the fullest expression of biblical faith. The lack of a loving relationship with the Lord is a sure indication that one has not yet been reconciled to him.

EARNED REWARD OR GRACIOUS GIFT?

We have already noted that Islam does not recognize man's sin nature and need for a Savior. The Muslim believes he is able, through careful and obedient participation in the obligations of Islam, to achieve a level of personal righteousness that will qualify him for the earned reward of an afterlife in eternal paradise. But Allah is not obligated to bestow this reward. Assignment to Muslim paradise is only a possibility, never a certainty. The only way to ensure entry into the eternal garden, according to Islam, is through death while participating in jihad against unbelievers (Sura 3:146–48).

By contrast, the forgiveness offered by Yahweh is a free, sure, and gracious gift to any man who is drawn by him and to him in heartfelt confession of moral failure. Man must depend completely on the perfect sacrifice of Christ to receive admission into the eternal presence of God.

The love of Allah is said to be demonstrated only toward those who act in accordance with his defined will. But the love of Yahweh reaches out proactively to reclaim those who go astray, taking the necessary action to revive their dead hearts and calling them to new life in him. The vengeance of Allah in the form of a curse is uncompromising and terrible, meted out without pardon to those who he has determined will be condemned; but Yahweh tempers his wrath with mercy, demonstrating long-suffering patience and tenderheartedness.

Using both table 23 and the previous tables, we are able to set a clear standard of deity in positive terms, as he has been understood by biblical Christianity for centuries before and since Muhammad.

The Westminster Confession of Faith, a document composed between 1643 and 1647, is unparalleled in its depth and completeness in describing this concept:

There is but one only, living, and true God, who is infinite in being and perfection, a most pure spirit, invisible, without body, parts, or passions; immutable, immense, eternal, incomprehensible, almighty, most

107

TABLE 23 Additional attributes of the biblical Yahweh

Attribute	Excerpt	Reference
A Spirit	"God is Spirit."	John 4:24
Infinite, eternal, unchangeable	" 'Do not I fill heaven and earth?' declares the LORD."	Jer. 23:24
in being	". . . who was, and is, and is to come!"	Rev. 4:8
in wisdom	"His understanding has no limit."	Ps. 147:5
in power	"I am God Almighty."	Gen. 17:1
in holiness	"I will sing praise to you . . . O Holy One of Israel."	Ps. 71:22
in justice	". . . without injustice; Righteous and upright is He."	Deut. 32:4 NKJV
in goodness	"The LORD is good; His mercy is everlasting."	Ps. 100:5 NKJV
in truth	"Just and true are your ways, King of the ages."	Rev. 15:3
	"The judgment of God is according to truth."	Rom. 2:2 NKJV
	". . . abounding in goodness and truth."	Ex. 34:6 NKJV
Manifested as Father, Son, Holy Spirit	"He [Jesus] saw the Spirit of God descending like a dove and alighting upon Him. And suddenly a voice came from heaven, saying, 'This is my Beloved Son.' "	Matt. 3:16–17 NKJV
	"The grace of the Lord Jesus Christ, and the love of God . . ."	2 Cor. 13:14
	". . . just as you [God the Father] are in me [Jesus] and I am in you."	John 17:21
	"Through him [Jesus] we both have access to the Father by one Spirit."	Eph. 2:18
	"We beheld His [Jesus'] glory, the glory as of the only begotten of the Father, full of grace and truth."	John 1:14–18 NKJV
	". . . spoken to us by His Son . . . the express image of His person."	Heb. 1:2–3 NKJV
	"He [Jesus] is the image of the invisible God, the firstborn over all creation."	Col. 1:15
	"The Spirit of Truth who proceeds from the Father, He will testify of Me [Jesus]."	John 15:26 NKJV
Savior	"For I am the LORD, your God, the Holy One of Israel, your Savior."	Isa. 43:3

TABLE 23 (*continued*)

Attribute	Excerpt	Reference
	"All mankind will know that I, the LORD, am your Savior, your Redeemer . . ."	Isa. 49:26
	"So he became their Savior."	Isa. 63:8
	"According to His mercy He saved us."	Titus 3:5 NKJV
	"Grow in the grace and knowledge of our Lord and Savior Jesus Christ."	2 Peter 3:18
	"We have seen and testify that the Father has sent his Son to be the Savior of the world."	I John 4:14
	". . . provide atonement for our sins . . ."	Ps. 79:9 NKJV
Redeemer	"the LORD, your Redeemer"	Isa. 48:17 NKJV
	"I know that my Redeemer lives."	Job 19:25
	"The LORD redeems the soul of His servants."	Ps. 34:22 NKJV
	"God will redeem my soul."	Ps. 49:15 NKJV
Unsearchable	"How unsearchable are His judgments and His ways past finding out!"	Rom. 11:33–34 NKJV
	"His understanding is unsearchable."	Isa. 40:28 NKJV
Unchangeable	"Has He spoken, and will He not make it good?"	Num. 23:19 NKJV
Unequaled	" 'Who is my equal?' says the Holy One."	Isa. 40:13–25
Omnipresent	"Where can I go from your Spirit? Where can I flee from Your presence?"	Ps. 139:7–12
Holy	"Be holy because I, the LORD your God, am holy."	Lev. 19:2
Impartial, just	". . . the Father, who without partiality judges . . ."	I Peter 1:17 NKJV
Long-suffering	"The LORD, the LORD God, merciful and gracious, long-suffering, and abounding in goodness and truth."	Ex. 34:6–7 NKJV
Loving	"God is love, and he who abides in love abides in God, and God in him."	I John 4:8, 16 NKJV
Truthful	". . . the truth that leads to godliness— a faith and knowledge resting on the hope of eternal life, which God, who does not lie, promised . . ."	Titus 1:1–2
Faithful	". . . the faithful God who keeps covenant and mercy for a thousand generations . . ."	Deut. 7:9 NKJV

109

TABLE 23 (*continued*)

Attribute	Excerpt	Reference
Gracious	"The LORD is gracious and full of compassion."	Ps. 111:4 NKJV
Good	"Oh, that men would give thanks to the LORD for His goodness, and for His wonderful works."	Ps. 107:8 NKJV
Light	"The LORD is my light and my salvation."	Ps. 27:1 NKJV
	". . . who lives in unapproachable light."	1 Tim. 6:16
Righteous	"Righteousness and justice are the foundation of your throne."	Ps. 89:14

wise, most holy, most free, most absolute; working all things according to the counsel of His own immutable and most righteous will; for His own glory; most loving, gracious, merciful, long-suffering, abundant in goodness and truth, forgiving iniquity, transgression, and sin; the rewarder of them that diligently seek Him; and withal, most just, and terrible in His judgments, hating all sin, and who will by no means clear the guilty. . . .

In the unity of the Godhead there be three persons, of one substance, power, and eternity; God the Father, God the Son, and God the Holy Ghost [Spirit]: the Father is of none, neither begotten, nor proceeding; the Son is eternally begotten of the Father; the Holy Ghost eternally proceeding from the Father and the Son.[14]

This is indeed a great mystery, but one that can be conceptualized. The character and Being of Yahweh overflow with ideological magnificence. The Holy Bible, with all its superlatives, gives us an astonishing glimpse of him. This image is so overwhelming that we can only fall face-down, as the prophet Ezekiel did in Ezekiel 1:28, in worship and adoration.

SIMILARITIES TO ALLAH?

One may look at the Westminster Confession's description and say, "But wait! Some of those descriptions sound like Allah. How about 'without passions,' 'incomprehensible,' 'the rewarder of them that diligently seek Him'? Isn't that a lot like Islam?"

Again, we must define terms. The use of the term *passions* in biblical Christianity most often means extreme emotion, which can override reason and cause dismay within the self and among others. In Islamic theology, *passion* refers to emotion in general. Allah has no feelings *at all*. He reveals his will to men not because he has any emotional attachment to them, but because men are his slaves and must bring themselves into submission to him. To assign emotion to him would be to weaken him, which is blasphemous.

Is the biblical Yahweh incomprehensible? Certainly, to man's finite mentality. Jesus advised his followers to receive the kingdom of God as a child does (Mark 10:15)—with the trusting simplicity and open candor that little ones display in abundance.

That the Triune God rewards those who seek him is not the same as saying that he loves only those who love him first, or that salvation is a reward based on man's personal effort. On the contrary, he promises men that if they seek him, they will find him (Deut. 4:29; Isa. 55:6; Matt. 7:7–8). This is an affirmation of his eagerness to fellowship with man.

111

Unique Attributes of Yahweh

Several particular biblical attributes of Yahweh deserve special consideration inasmuch as they are remarkably absent in Islamic thought. There are five:

- The fatherhood of Yahweh
- His role as Savior-Redeemer
- His divine love
- His divine justice
- The harmony within his character

The idea of Yahweh as a Divine Father is firmly rooted in Old Testament theology and is most clearly demonstrated during the earthly ministry of Jesus Christ. Jesus startled the multitudes by addressing Yahweh as "Abba," the Aramaic equivalent of "Papa." This loving informality seemed almost impertinent to the pious Pharisees. Yet it was not disrespectful; it signified the epitome of confident familiarity.

By identifying Yahweh as his Father, Jesus was demonstrating a great truth—that God is approachable and hears the appeal of a humble heart, as a human father keeps an attentive ear to the cries of his children. We have a Holy Parent who is always available and always has time for us. What a comfort this is in times of sorrow, pain, and despair! What a joy this is in times of great praise and pleasure!

As our Heavenly Father, he has taken on the role of our "kinsman-redeemer," another ancient concept found in the Holy Bible. Among the very early Hebrews, it was imperative that the family name be preserved and that land and property be secured for future generations. If a family member was orphaned or widowed, or in other extreme circumstances, he or she would appeal to a close male relative for assistance. If the relative accepted the responsibility, he paid any outstanding debts, repurchased or assumed ownership of any holdings, or bought back the family member from slavery if necessary. That responsible relative became the "kinsman-redeemer"—essentially a legal guardian—for the family member in difficulty. This position was often assumed at great personal sacrifice to the kinsman-redeemer. It is beautifully illustrated in the biblical book of Ruth (see text footnotes in the *Reformation Study Bible*, p. 370).

Yahweh has assumed this role for his people. Instead of redeeming property or possessions, he purchases his children's freedom from sin and condemnation. As the perfect Savior of mankind, he is the only one worthy or able to take on such a task.

Why would he have to? Because of the next two attributes: his divine love and justice.

Yahweh is righteous. He alone has defined and established what is right and true. It is against his nature to do anything contrary to his Truth. His standards are moral absolutes, his character is holy, and only perfection may stand in his presence.

His justice requires that sin be punished. His love begs that sinners be shown mercy. How can the two be reconciled? Only through his own intervention, which alone is able to satisfy both divine laws. In Christ, perfect love and perfect justice are both fulfilled.

This is the ultimate harmony. In Yahweh, these characteristics are not in conflict, but complement each other in a way that can only be described as divine. The cross achieves it; the resurrection confirms it. No dissonance can be heard in the symphony of salvation he has written.

With this in our minds and hearts, let's look at the Qur'anic Allah again. The portrait of deity painted in table 24 bears no resemblance to the biblical Triune God.

To enumerate the points more precisely:

- The Qur'anic Allah is not wholly good. He is also the creator and manipulator of evil, practicing deceit if he pleases, in order to impose his autocratic will. In twenty passages of the Qur'an, it is said that Allah leads people astray.
- The Qur'anic Allah is not known as a father, nor does he have a son, nor does he bring man into his family by faith. He does not manifest himself in the Holy Spirit. Therefore, without the fatherhood of God, the true brotherhood of man is impossible.
- The Qur'anic Allah does not watch over man with tenderness and concern, but watches man as a guard watches prisoners. He protects only those who demonstrate absolute obedience to his ritualistic commands.
- The Qur'anic Allah does not forgive all sin, even after repeated appeals. Conversely, he may forgive grievous sin if he wishes, or condemn someone for merely minor offenses. He is not obligated to adhere to any standard of moral justice. He changed the law on more than one occasion for the Prophet alone.
- The Qur'anic Allah has no desires, not even that men should believe in him. Therefore, man's devotion and behavior is meaningless because it serves no useful divine purpose.

114

TABLE 24   Additional attributes of Allah

Attribute	Excerpt	Sura
Creator, Sustainer of all things, good and evil	"Say: 'Who is the Lord and Sustainer of the heavens and the earth?' "	13:16; 7:54
	"... Who made constellations in the skies."	25:61
	"... created man: He has taught him speech."	55:3–4
	"Allah has created you and your handiwork [carved idols]."	37:96; 15:29–43
Not triune	"Do not say 'Trinity': desist; it will be better for you ..."	4:171
	"He is just One Allah."	16:51
	"It is not befitting to (the majesty of) Allah that He should beget a son."	19:35
	"No son did Allah beget."	23:91
	"No partner has He ..."	6.163
Watchful guardian	"Your Lord is [as a Guardian] on a watch tower."	89:14
	"He is the One that hears and knows (all things)."	21:4
Protector of believers only	"So establish regular Prayer, give regular Charity, and hold fast to Allah! He is your Protector."	22:78
	"Allah is the Protector of those who have faith."	2:257
Self-sufficient	"Allah is He (that is) free of all wants."	31:26
Withholds forgiveness	"He forgives whom He pleases, and punishes whom He pleases."	2:284
	"Allah is Oft-forgiving, most Merciful."	3:129
	"Allah does not forgive (the sin of) joining other gods with Him."	4:116
	"If you ask seventy times for their forgiveness, Allah will not forgive them."	9:80
Wills disunity	"(His plan is) to test you in what He has given you."	5:48
Only one to be invoked	"If anyone invokes, besides Allah, any other god, he has no authority."	23:117
	"They can have no (real) Faith, until they make you judge in all disputes between them."	4:65
	"(The unbelievers) plotted and planned, and Allah too planned."	3:54

TABLE 24   (*continued*)

Attribute	Excerpt	Sura
	"We test you by evil and by good . . ."	21:35
Abrogates law for the Prophet	"Prophet! Why do you hold to be forbidden that which Allah has made lawful to thee?"	66:1–2
	". . . any believing woman who dedicates her soul to the Prophet if the prophet wishes to wed her;—this only for you, and not for the Believers (at large) . . ."	33:50
Autocratic and uncompromising	"For your Lord is quick in punishment."	6:165
	". . . then would you find none to plead your affair in that matter as against Us."	17:86
	"Thus Allah leaves to stray whom He pleases . . . none can know the forces of your Lord, except He."	74:31
	". . . when (once) Allah wills a people's punishment, there can be no turning it back."	13:11
	"Say 'He has power to send calamities on you.' "	6:65
	"When We decide to destroy a population . . . the word is proved true against them: then (it is) We destroy them utterly."	17:16
Loves those who love him first	"Say: 'If you do love Allah, follow me. Allah will love you.' "	3:31–32
Helps those who help themselves first	"Never will Allah change the condition of a people until they change it themselves."	13:11

- The Qur'anic Allah is not a redeemer or savior. Man must strive to save himself through acts of total submission to Qur'anic authority. Man can never be sure of his entry to paradise in the hereafter unless he dies in battle for Islam.
- The Qur'anic Allah is not consistent in character. His will is arbitrary and capricious. Man can never rest in his promises or be certain of his word.

116

Names of Allah

Allah is addressed, in the Qur'an and in the Hadith, by 99 "Glorious Names," which illuminate him more fully. They include titles such as "The Just," "The Truth," and "The Compassionate"—but these words do not carry the same meanings in Islam as they do in biblical theology. The attitude of Allah in exhibiting these characteristics is like that of an overpowering warrior-king, showing kindness to those he has vanquished by refraining from totally annihilating them. This can hardly be called "compassion."

Other names on the list include "The Contriver," "The Afflicter," "The Accounter" (Reckoner), "The Humiliator," "The Killer at His Will" (Al-Mumit), "The Seizer," and "The Over-Powering One." These titles clearly identify Allah as a god of conquest and compulsion.

What's in a Name?

Names mean a great deal in all three faith traditions: Judaism, Christianity, and Islam. A scan through the Bible reveals numerous examples of names being assigned based on personality traits, historical events, prophetic insight, and spiritual rebirth. Yahweh himself revealed his divine name to Moses and told him, " 'This is my name forever, the name by which I am to be remembered from generation to generation' " (Ex. 3:15). The Hebrew name *Yahweh* means "I was, I am, I will be." It uses all three tenses, revealing the Triune God's eternality and constancy.

Allah is a specific Arabic name. Although it is commonly translated as "the God," that is not entirely accurate. The name *Al-ilah* had been known in pre-Islamic Arabia as the proper name for one of the chief gods in the Arabic pantheon. His idol, along with approximately 360 others, was housed in the Ka'aba in Mecca long before Muhammad designated him as the source of his revelations. Allah was well known among all the tribes on the Arabian peninsula during the seventh century.

GOD'S PURPOSE FOR MAN

Allah is completely transcendent and distant—physically, spiritually, and emotionally. A Muslim is this god's slave, not his child. What is Allah's purpose for man? That he submit to him. Why? So that men might attain prosperity and power in this life and enter the sensual garden of delights in paradise after death. To what end? This is unknown, since Allah needs nothing, wants nothing, expects nothing.

Writes Michael Sells, "In many mystical theologies, unity involves knowing and seeing nothing but the one deity, or arriving at a point where a person's own existence actually passes away into the infinite reaches of that one God that is all that truly is."[15] This resembles a type of pantheistic mysticism. Suras 28:88; 6:60, 72; 10:45–46 all express the idea that everything that exists, including human beings, will ultimately return to Allah. "In some sense it could be argued that humankind waits to be erased in the indivisibility of the Creator; the only reality."[16] How does this affect the individual Muslim? Farid Esack shares his own personal musings about Allah during his pilgrimage to Mecca: "Many of us who do take Allah seriously have been desperate for answers to questions that tear at our selves, and do not understand why He watches us being destroyed by the absence of answers."[17] As Esack approaches the holy

118

shrine from the surrounding countryside, he continues, "If only I, too, I thought, could descend into a seemingly barren self and cause a new being to come forth from a desolate soul." He proceeds to join the circumambulations around the Ka'bah, reading the prescribed recitations. He writes, "However desperately needed, there was still no self-expression or erratic, even frenzied, crying from a mutilated self."

When finally reaching the door of the shrine, he confesses:

I wept bitterly, for my past, present and future, I wept for what I believed was an existence in mud and actually hoped that someone would come from inside the door.

I sat there, drained and frightened, after what appeared to be hours of choking in "humiliated in Your presence." With my emptiness and nothingness complete, I stumbled away, repeating to myself: "What did He have in mind to subject me to this apparently divine indifference?"

In sum, he observes, "I had been desperate to make sense of Islam and my relationship with Allah and now, for the first time, everything seemed so perfectly pointless."

To our knowledge, this gentleman remains a Muslim and has come to an acceptance of spiritual life with this refrain: "The presence of Allah in the world and in my life, whatever else it may be, is real enough for me to believe in."[18] To the biblical Christian, this statement has the desolate ring of resignation—and it is a sad, hollow sound.

By contrast, what is Yahweh's chief purpose for man? That man glorify him and enjoy him forever! (Westminster

Shorter Catechism, Q. 1). Why? Because it is his good pleasure that his spiritual children should have fellowship with him. To what end? To celebrate and spend eternity in joyful fellowship together.

Says Samuel Zwemer of the Islamic and biblical Christian ideas of the Godhead, "No parliament of religions can reconcile such fundamental and deep-rooted differences."[19]

PUBLIC PIETY

Another interesting phenomenon is that while Muslims maintain that Allah is completely transcendent, Muslim culture proceeds as though he were immanent. This is not the immanence of spiritually sensing the comfort of his presence, but the conviction that he constantly watches over everything Muslims say, do, and think. These "deeds" are monitored and documented for use in the Day of Judgment (Sura 99:6–8).

Christians tend to err on the opposite side of the spectrum. While maintaining that God is immanent—comforting and guiding believers through the active presence of the Holy Spirit—we often tend to live as if he were totally transcendent. We do not "pray continually" as Paul exhorted us in 1 Thessalonians 5:17, nor do we regularly appeal to him first in order to keep us on the right path in times of confusion or dismay as in Proverbs 3:6. We do not adorn our speech or our conduct with regular references to him in accordance with Ephesians 5:29, nor do we convey the impression that he is relevant in everyday life. We confess this to our own sorrow and shame.

These tendencies lead to ironic public perceptions. Muslims are seen by Christians as being religious fanatics because their environment is replete with references to Allah in speech, writing, art, etc. Christians are seen by Muslims as being religious apathetics, relegating God to Sunday-morning sermons and dinner prayers. Yet neither view is accurate.

The constant evocation of Allah in Muslim culture is meant to continually remind believers of their obligations before him and to maintain public pressure to be in visible total submission at all times. Thus, in spite of the appearance of piety, it is more a form of "pietism." Farid Esack writes:

> The vast majority of Muslims . . . experience Allah only via the trappings of reified Islam and often as an afterthought; an all-powerful being to be invoked in appendages to everyday speech: *insha Allah* (God willing), *masha Allah* (as God pleased), or when disaster strikes.[20]

> It is . . . possible to complete all one's legal obligations in respect of the prayers and bypass Allah completely. We are able to rush through the "whole thing" in a few minutes flat to get it over with.[21]

By contrast, the seeming lack of public manifestations of faith among biblical Christians within the general population often belies a deeper spirituality. Since faith is regarded as a personal relationship, it is often demonstrated in quieter and less flamboyant ways within the community. Relationships are gentle things, to be nourished by shared experiences, not things to be trumpeted and paraded in misguided veneration.

So, although hypocrisy is not a stranger to either faith, neither is true devotion. But there are greater dangers of false piety in a system that heavily relies on publicly enforced behaviors to maintain or judge the quality of a believer's faith. Jesus warns us, " 'Be careful not to do your "acts of righteousness" before men, to be seen by them' " (Matt. 6:1–18).

CONCLUSION

We are left to choose from two different conclusions about the identities of Allah and Yahweh.

1. Allah and Yahweh are the same deity, although revealed to Muslims and Christians in antithetical terms, and demonstrating completely different ultimate purposes.
2. Allah and Yahweh are separate deities—one false and one true—with attributes that cannot be reconciled and purposes that are in opposition.

The first choice is logically indefensible. The second is literally undeniable.

Although Sura 29:46–48 asserts that Christians and Muslims worship the same deity, it is clear that the concepts of the Godhead held by each faith are vastly different. Divine Truth does not contradict itself this way. Therefore, we must reject the first conclusion.

The second conclusion, although unpopular in today's "politically correct" climate, must be admitted: Yahweh and Allah are not the same deity. Many Muslims, especially those in positions of power, already know this. That is why Jews and Christians are not treated as "brothers in faith" in countries under Islamic law. Worship and free expression of both Judaism and Christianity are often made more difficult in these nations through the enforcement of financial penalties and taxes, implementation of regulations meant to discourage or prohibit the building or repairing of worship facilities, or other tactics, both subtle and overt, designed to slow or eliminate the practice of other faiths.

This makes no sense if the Qur'anic Allah is the same deity as the biblical Yahweh. Shouldn't Muslims welcome the "striving" of other peoples toward him?

A more dramatic example of the exclusivity of the name of Allah is found in present-day Malaysia. Before the government was under Islamic law, Muslims encouraged Malaysian Christians to use *Allah* to address God, insisting that it was a generic name for the One True God. After Muslims assumed political power, however, they made it illegal for Christians to use the word *Allah* in reference to the Christian God.

Muslims know what media pundits do not—that Allah is a *very particular Islamic god,* not to be confused with any other and not to be worshiped in any other way than that outlined in the Noble Qur'an.

Authors Ergun and Emir Caner, former Muslims who have come to know Jesus as Lord and have embraced biblical Christianity, report a recent encounter with an Islamic gentleman in a public forum. When they pointedly asked this Muslim man if Allah and Jehovah (Yahweh) were the same deity, the gentleman replied, "No, of course not." He was not just giving his personal opinion—this is the Islamic understanding of the issue.[22]

OFF COURSE

Ideas have consequences. Devotion to a mind-numbing concept of God must lead men into ultimate error. The reli-

123

gious-course readings about Allah in the Noble Qur'an won't keep a follower on the original and true course toward the God of the "people of the Book," whose name is Yahweh.

The consequence is devastating—a journey and destination straying further and further from Divine Truth. Only the Heavenly Father's beacon of light, the gospel of Christ, charged with the fire of the Holy Spirit, can set such a traveler back on course.

"A Prayer for the Muslim World"
(CONTINUED)

. . . Father,
the hour has come;
glorify thy Son in the Muslim world,
and fulfill through him
the prayer
of Abraham thy friend,
"O, that Ishmael might live
before thee."
For Jesus' sake.
Amen.[23]

6

QUR'ANIC AND BIBLICAL
LIVING: LAW AND GRACE

Islam possesses a religious law called al-Shari'ah in Arabic which governs the life of Muslims and which Muslims consider to be the embodiment of the Will of God. The Shari'ah is contained in principle in the Qur'an as elaborated and complemented by the Sunnah. On the basis of these principles the schools of law which are followed by all Muslims to this day were developed early in Islamic history. The Law, while being rooted in the sources of the Islamic revelation, is a living body of law which caters to the needs of Islamic society.[1]

For what the law was powerless to do in that it was weakened by the sinful nature, God did by sending his own Son in the likeness of sinful man to be a sin offering. And so he condemned sin in sinful man, in order that the righteous requirements of the law might be fully met in us, who do not live according to the sinful nature but according to the Spirit. (Rom. 8:3–4)

The goal of Muslim cultural expansion is the imposition of Islamic law over all human populations. The goal of Christian gospel proclamation is the introduction of biblical grace into all human hearts. One seeks to impose man-made control externally; the other seeks God's control internally. One seeks human subjugation; the other pursues divine sanctification. In short, two very different perspectives about the intersection between spiritual and secular life emerge when we survey the belief systems of Qur'anic Islam and biblical Christianity.

WHAT EXACTLY IS SHARI'AH?

The fabric of any Muslim nation is woven with the tough legal cord of "shari'ah," derived from the Noble Qur'an, Sunnah, and Hadith. The establishment and enforcement of the tenets of Islam over all parameters of civil and social life furthers the expectation that Islam will one day conquer the world and be a truly "global civilization."

Table 25 lists samples of the types of laws found in the Noble Qur'an. Being a Muslim goes beyond the observance of the five pillars or the acceptance of the articles of the faith regarding Allah, angels, the Day of Judgment, etc. Submission to civil man-made law is part and parcel of the system. Public and private life is tightly regulated in nations embracing shari'ah as their legal system. This regulation enforces Islam's vision of righteousness and total submission to Allah.

One interesting thing about this table is the preponderance of suras that are drawn from the longer, chronologically later recitations of Muhammad. There is a simple reason for this: these revelations were delivered by Muhammad after his victorious return to Mecca. His rise to political

TABLE 25 Sample laws in the Noble Qur'an

Subject	Excerpt	Sura
Ablutions	"When you prepare for prayer, wash your faces and your hands (and arms) to the elbows; rub your heads (with water); and (wash) your feet to the ankles."	5:6
Penalty for adultery	"The woman and the man guilty of adultery or fornication,—flog each of them with a hundred stripes: let not compassion move you in their case."	24:2
No appeal of legal decisions	"It is not fitting for a Believer, man or woman, when a matter has been decided by Allah and His Messenger, to have any option about their decision."	33:36
Distribution of booty	"And know that out of all the booty that you may acquire (in war), a fifth share is assigned to Allah,—and to the Messenger, and to near relatives, orphans, the needy, and the wayfarer."	8:41
Divorce and remarriage	"So if a husband divorces his wife (irrevocably), he cannot, after that, re-marry her until after she has married another husband and he has divorced her."	2:230
Disloyalty of wives	"As to those women on whose part you fear disloyalty and ill-conduct, admonish them (first), (next), refuse to share their beds, (and last) beat them (lightly)."	4:34
Fasting	"Fasting is prescribed to you as it was prescribed to those before you, that you may (learn) self-restraint . . . for a fixed number of days."	2:183–84
Jihad	"Fighting is prescribed for you, and you dislike it. But it is possible that you dislike a thing which is good for you."	2:216
Food	"He has only forbidden you dead meat, and blood, and the flesh of swine, and that on which any other name has been invoked besides that of Allah."	2:173
Inheritance	"Allah (thus) directs you as regards your children's (inheritance): to the male, a portion equal to that of two females: if only daughters, two or more, their share is two-thirds of the inheritance; if only one, her share is a half."	4:11

129

TABLE 25 *(continued)*

Subject	Excerpt	Sura
Recompense for injury	"The recompense for an injury is an injury equal thereto (in degree)."	42:40
Lewdness in women	"If any of your women are guilty of lewdness, take the evidence of four (reliable) witnesses from amongst you against them; and if they testify, confine them to houses until death do claim them."	4:15
Murder and compensation	"The law of equality is prescribed to you in cases of murder: the free for the free, the slave for the slave, the woman for the woman. But if any remission is made by the brother of the slain, then grant any reasonable demand, and compensate him with handsome gratitude."	2:178
Pilgrimage to Mecca	". . . the Station of Abraham; whoever enters it attains security; pilgrimage thereto is a duty men owe to Allah."	3:97
Punishment for theft	"As to the thief, male or female, cut off his or her hands: a punishment by way of example, from Allah, for their crime: and Allah is Exalted in Power."	5:38
Punishment for those who war against the Prophet	"The punishment of those who wage war against Allah and His Messenger . . . is: execution, or crucifixion, or the cutting off of hands and feet from opposite sides, or exile from the land."	5:33

prominence forced him to develop a way of governing and controlling the population. Consequently and conveniently, the suras became more and more directed toward legal pronouncements and reinforced the legally binding authority of the Prophet.

As Muhammad's career advanced, the ritual core of Islam was more fully articulated within the Qur'an. Of the "five pillars" of Islamic practice, three were discussed in the early Meccan Suras: the affirmation of the oneness of God, the ritual prayer (salat), and the obligation to give a pure offering (zakat) of one's wealth to those in need. In later Suras, the number of prayers required per day was fixed at five and the orientation of the prayers was set toward the shrine of the Ka'aba in Mecca; the obligation for fasting during the month of Ramadan (the month the initial Qur'anic revelations are believed to have been sent down to Muhammad) was enjoined on all able adult Muslims; and, finally, the Islamic pilgrimage or hajj, which contained many of the elements of pre-Islamic pilgrimage activities around Mecca, was ordained for all Muslims capable of it.[2]

These themes, and others, were further expanded upon in the Hadith. As the Muslim forces assumed control of more territory, the Islamic judicial system became increasingly repressive to non-Muslims. Blatant inequities were codified. For instance, according to Hadiths recorded in the nine-volume work entitled *The Translation of the Meaning of Sahih Al-Bukhari,* and reported in Robert Morey's book *The Islamic Invasion* (pp. 199, 201), the testimony of a non-Muslim is not valid against a Muslim (vol. 3:525–26); Muslims cannot be executed for murdering "infidels," which constitute anyone outside of Islam (vol. 4:283; vol. 9:50); and Muslims are ordered to kill any fellow Muslim who discards Islam (vol. 4:160; vol. 5:630; and others throughout vol. 9).

Religious discrimination is maintained to this day. Several contemporary examples of edicts being pronounced by Muslim clerics against specific individuals come quickly to mind, the most noted being the "hit" ordered on the author Salman Rushdie for his novel *The Satanic Verses.* If Rushdie had been assassinated in any Islamic country, his murderer would have been lauded and commended as a champion of Islam.

This also explains the high regard of some Muslims for suicide bombers. To them, these young people are martyrs for the faith. They further the expansion of Islam by eliminating infidels. In addition, they are the only Muslims who are guaranteed life after death in Islamic paradise. The Ayatollah Khomeini once said that "the purest joy in Islam is to kill and be killed for Allah."[3]

Though we are reluctant to characterize Islamic fanaticism as anything but an extreme or aberrant form of Islam, the truth is that it follows from an honest and forthright interpretation of fundamental Qur'anic texts. To escape the obvious conclusion that Islamic law sanctions violence, one would have to blatantly overlook or completely eliminate essential sections of the Noble Qur'an.

TRUE BIBLICAL LAW

Human beings are the least humble of all creatures. We are born with exalted egos and overwhelming desire to assert ourselves at the expense of others. Observe any group of two year olds at play, and this trait is supremely evident. It is not learned; it is inborn.

Before any deed is done, our characters are already tainted with our overinflated self-consciousness. From the moment we take our first breath, we are selfish, self-centered, self-absorbed, and self-pitying. Satisfaction of the ever-present and insatiable "self" becomes our continual goal.

In order to take root and survive, civilization must establish some way to restrain the individual self-seeking egos of

132

its people. The restraint of "self" can come from two sources: externally applied law and internally strengthened conscience. Through these methods, the implanted moral law can be enforced and reinforced.

The biblical Triune God graciously gave both to us. To Moses, he revealed the external law, summed up succinctly in the Ten Commandments, or Decalogue.

THE TEN COMMANDMENTS
(RECORDED IN DEUT. 5:6–22)

"I am the LORD your God, who brought you out of Egypt, out of the land of slavery.

"You shall have no other gods before me.

"You shall not make for yourself an idol in the form of anything in heaven above or on the earth beneath or in the waters below. You shall not bow down to them or worship them; for I, the LORD your God, am a jealous God, punishing the children for the sin of the fathers to the third and fourth generation of those who hate me, but showing love to thousands who love me and keep my commandments.

"You shall not misuse the name of the LORD your God, for the LORD will not hold anyone guiltless who misuses his name.

"Observe the Sabbath day by keeping it holy, as the LORD your God has commanded you. Six days you shall labor and do all your work, but the seventh day is a Sabbath to the LORD your God. On it you shall not do any work, neither you, nor your son or daughter, nor your manservant or maidservant, nor your ox, your donkey or any of your animals, nor the alien within your gates, so that your manservant and maidservant may rest, as you do. Remember that you were slaves in Egypt and that the LORD your God brought you out of there with a mighty hand and an outstretched arm. Therefore the LORD your God has commanded you to observe the Sabbath day.

"Honor your father and your mother, as the LORD your God has commanded you, so that you may live long and that it may go well with you in the land the LORD your God is giving you.

"You shall not murder.

"You shall not commit adultery.

"You shall not steal.

"You shall not give false testimony against your neighbor.

"You shall not covet your neighbor's wife. You shall not set your desire on your neighbor's house or land, his manservant or maidservant, his ox or donkey, or anything that belongs to your neighbor."

These are the commandments the LORD proclaimed in a loud voice to your whole assembly there on the mountain from out of the fire, the cloud and the deep darkness; and *he added nothing more*. Then he wrote them on two stone tablets and gave them to me. (Italics ours.)

The Torah (first five books of the Holy Bible) details further instructions regarding the application of these laws in specific circumstances. Other regulations address the proper presentation of offerings, direct the observation of sacred feasts, and designate clean and unclean foods and their preparation.

Still others deal with health and hygiene and helpful procedures for the diagnosis of disease. Table 26 lists biblical passages that elucidate the value of God's law to his people.

The law given to the Israelites by Yahweh through Moses was straight from his heart. It was not just a list of rules and regulations, but transmitted a deeper meaning. It outlined the perfection of character and Being to be found in the Promised One. The goal of the law of Moses was to highlight our inability to achieve this perfection on our own, as Paul wrote in his letter to the Romans: "Therefore no one will be declared righteous in his sight by observing the law; rather, through the law we become conscious of sin" (Rom. 3:20).

Yehia Sa'a, in his book *All That the Prophets Have Spoken,* describes the process in this way:

> Most people will agree that they are sinners. However, few will readily admit that they are helpless sinners. There is a big difference.
>
> Sinners believe that there is something they can do to make themselves acceptable to God. They may believe that God wants them to observe the Ten Commandments. Or they may believe that attending religious meetings, praying faithfully, fasting, going on pilgrimages, giving to charity or being nice to their neighbors will make them pleasing to God.
>
> The notion that a person's good can outweigh his bad, and therefore merit God's acceptance is totally foreign to the Bible. To do good is commendable, but the Scripture teaches that none of these deeds can restore our broken relationship with God. We have a deep problem we can't get rid of—it's the sin condition.

135

TABLE 26 Law in the Holy Bible

Excerpt	Reference
"But his delight is in the law of the LORD, and on his law he meditates day and night."	Ps. 1:2
"Blessed are they whose ways are blameless, who walk according to the law of the LORD."	Ps. 119:1
"My son, if you accept my words and store up my commands within you, . . . then you will understand the fear of the LORD and find the knowledge of God."	Prov. 2:1–5
"To the law and to the testimony! If they do not speak according to this word, they have no light of dawn."	Isa. 8:20
"Hear me, you who know what is right, you people who have my law in your hearts."	Isa. 51:7
"I will put my law in their minds and write it on their hearts. I will be their God, and they will be my people."	Jer. 31:33
"Do not think that I [Jesus] have come to abolish the Law or the Prophets; I have not come to abolish them but to fulfill them."	Matt. 5:17
"So in everything, do to others what you would have them do to you, for this sums up the Law and the Prophets."	Matt. 7:12
"The crowds were amazed at his [Jesus'] teaching, because he taught as one who had authority."	Matt. 7:28–29
"Jesus replied: ' "Love the Lord your God with all your heart and with all your soul and with all your mind." This is the first and greatest commandment. And the second is like it: "Love your neighbor as yourself." All the Law and the Prophets hang on these two commandments.' "	Matt. 22:37–40
"But you have neglected the more important matters of the law—justice, mercy and faithfulness."	Matt. 23:23
"Jesus replied, 'And you experts in the law, woe to you, because you load people down with burdens they can hardly carry.' "	Luke 11:46
"Everything must be fulfilled that is written about me [Jesus] in the Law of Moses, the Prophets and the Psalms."	Luke 24:44
"For the law was given through Moses; grace and truth came through Jesus Christ."	John 1:17
"We have found the one Moses wrote about in the Law, and about whom the prophets also wrote—Jesus of Nazareth, the son of Joseph."	John 1:45
"They show that the requirements of the law are written on their hearts, their consciences also bearing witness."	Rom. 2:15

QUR'ANIC AND BIBLICAL LIVING: LAW AND GRACE

TABLE 26   *(continued)*

Excerpt	Reference
"But now a righteousness from God, apart from law, has been made known, to which the Law and the Prophets testify. This righteousness from God comes through faith in Jesus Christ."	Rom. 3:21–22
"For we maintain that a man is justified by faith apart from observing the law."	Rom. 3:28
"For sin shall not be your master, because you are not under law, but under grace."	Rom. 6:14
"He who loves his fellowman has fulfilled the law."	Rom. 13:8
"What, then, was the purpose of the law? It was added because of transgressions until the Seed to whom the promise referred had come."	Gal. 3:19
"You who are trying to be justified by law have been alienated from Christ; you have fallen away from grace."	Gal. 5:4
"Carry each other's burdens, and in this way you will fulfill the law of Christ."	Gal. 6:2
"We also know that law is made not for the righteous, but for lawbreakers and rebels, the ungodly and sinful."	I Tim. 1:9
"The law is only a shadow of the good things that are coming—not the realities themselves."	Heb. 10:1
"For whoever keeps the whole law and yet stumbles at just one point is guilty of breaking all of it."	James 2:10

On the other hand, a helpless sinner knows there is nothing he can do to make himself acceptable to God.[4]

BIBLICAL CHRISTIANS AND THE LAW

Antinomianism is the theological term meaning "against the law" or "anti-lawism." Antinomians believe that Christians are no longer under any obligation to obey the moral law of Yahweh. This is heresy contrary to the principles of true biblical Christianity. It is the result of confusing the doctrines of "justification" and "sanctification." R. C. Sproul writes in *Essential Truths of the Christian Faith*: "Justifica-

137

tion may be defined as that act by which unjust sinners are made right in the sight of a just and holy God. Justification by faith alone means justification by the righteousness or merit of Christ alone, not by our goodness or good deeds."[5]

On the other hand, to be sanctified is "to be made holy, or righteous. Sanctification is a process that begins the moment we become Christians. The process continues until death when the believer is made finally, fully, and forevermore righteous."[6]

Justification is a singular event; sanctification is an ongoing process. Justification is accomplished by the atoning death and resurrection of Christ, his righteousness applied to individuals as they are called to him in repentance and faith. Sanctification is accomplished by the work of the Holy Spirit, who indwells believers, consecrates them, and makes them "saints."

The task of the Holy Spirit is to implant the moral law in our minds, hearts, and souls in a new and vibrant way. The law of God becomes an internal guidance system, and believers are called to obey it at a higher standard than mere external observance. Consider carefully these words of Jesus Christ:

> You have heard that it was said to the people long ago, "Do not murder, and anyone who murders will be subject to judgment." But I tell you that anyone who is angry with his brother will be subject to judgment. Again, anyone who says to his brother, "Raca [empty head]," is answerable to the Sanhedrin. But anyone who says, "You fool!" will be in danger of the fire of hell. (Matt. 5:21–22)

> You have heard that it was said, "Do not commit adultery." But I tell you that anyone who looks at a

woman lustfully has already committed adultery with her in his heart. (Matt. 5:27–28)

Jesus is teaching a remarkable truth: we are as accountable for our emotions and thoughts as we are for our deeds. It is not just the commission of a particular behavior that is regarded as sin, but also the motivation of our hearts that leads to the act. Therefore, even if the deed is not carried out, the feeling or idea has already violated the law.

Control of our emotional state and thought life is a far more difficult task than just making sure that we look good to others. The biblical Triune God wants to clean the vessel inside and out. The moral law becomes the rudder of the boat, rather than the coat of paint on the hull.

Thus, far from being released from the obligation of the law, biblical Christians are divinely empowered by the grace of the Holy Spirit to honor it in a way that far surpasses the righteousness of the Pharisees (Matt. 23:5–7). Sproul writes, "All believers grow in faith by keeping God's holy commands—not to gain God's favor, but out of loving gratitude for the grace already bestowed on them through the work of Christ."[7]

MUSLIMS AND LEGALISM

The opposite of antinomianism is legalism. Essentially, this is the "adherence to the letter of the law to the exclusion of the spirit of the law."[8] Islam sincerely believes that man is capable of achieving personal righteousness by adherence to the letter of shari'ah law. As Michael Sells continues in *Approaching the Qur'an:* "The Qur'an does not propound a doctrine of the original or essential sinfulness of humanity. Human beings are not born sinful, but they are forgetful. This forgetfulness can be countered only by reminder (dhikr), which the Qur'an calls itself."[9]

But Islamic law goes beyond simple Qur'anic reminders. It is strict and strong—zealously enforced by Muslim clerics who are endowed with civil authority. It is often punitive and discriminatory. *Islam: A Global Civilization* tries to explain away Islam's use of punishment with this paragraph:

> Islamic laws are essentially preventative and are not based on harsh punishment except as a last measure. The faith of the Muslim causes him to have respect for the rights of others and Islamic Law is such that it prevents transgression from taking place in most instances. That is why what people consider to be harsh punishments are so rarely in need of being applied.[10]

Yet they are applied, and not infrequently. In fact, the public use of harsh measures motivates the rest of the population toward greater compliance. Michael Sells notes:

> The importance and usefulness of fear of punishment and desire for reward is a controversial issue in Islamic history. Some major theologians, such as Hasan al-Basri and al-Ghazali, believed that contemplation of the terrors of punishment and the bliss of rewards were essential to refining the human conscience.[11]

This shallow refinement of character lasts only as long as the threat is maintained. Such a method does not lead to true internal commitment to the principle behind the law, nor does it foster devotion to the law-giver. The human con-

140

science is not transformed by punitive measures. It must be wooed by love and grace.

REDEEMING BIBLICAL GRACE

Grace has most often been defined as "unmerited favor"—which, indeed, it is. But there is more to it than that. It is an active and dynamic quality, given to the biblical Christian as a gift. It infuses divine strength into his human spirit. It initiates and seals salvation, guides and ensures sanctification, promises and protects glorification.

When grace is poured out onto a believer, it soaks him through and through, anointing the will and taming the "self" in a way that externally applied law cannot. It is transforming and life-changing.

The Holy Bible has much to say about grace. Table 27 lists examples of this most important quality. Notice the variety of concepts that are paired with grace. It characterizes the throne of God Almighty and proceeds from him. It is abundant, full, rich, lavish, and sufficient. It goes hand in hand with wisdom, supplication, the gospel, the message, the Word, and the knowledge of Jesus Christ. Through it humble men receive salvation, an inheritance, a promise, righteousness, faith, love, gifts, a generous spirit, and the ability to converse pleasantly with others about God. It loves human weakness because then it may work powerfully and perfectly.

The Westminster Confession of Faith describes the believer in a "state of grace" as follows:

Although hypocrites and other unregenerate men may vainly deceive themselves with false hopes and car-

141

TABLE 27   Grace in the Holy Bible

Excerpt	Reference
"For the LORD God is a sun and shield; The LORD will give grace and glory."	Ps. 84:11 NKJV
"He mocks proud mockers but gives grace to the humble."	Prov. 3:34
"Those who cling to worthless idols forfeit the grace that could be theirs."	Jonah 2:8
"And I will pour out on the house of David and the inhabitants of Jerusalem a spirit of grace and supplication."	Zech. 12:10
"And the child [Jesus] grew and became strong; he was filled with wisdom, and the grace of God was upon him."	Luke 2:40
"From the fullness of his grace we have all received one blessing after another."	John 1:16
"With great power the apostles continued to testify to the resurrection of the Lord Jesus, and much grace was upon them all."	Acts 4:33
"When he arrived and saw the evidence of the grace of God, he was glad, and encouraged them all to remain true to the Lord with all their hearts."	Acts 11:23
"Many . . . followed Paul and Barnabas, who talked with them and urged them to continue in the grace of God."	Acts 13:43
"So Paul and Barnabas spent considerable time there, speaking boldly for the Lord, who confirmed the message of his grace by enabling them to do miraculous signs and wonders."	Acts 14:3
". . . the task of testifying to the gospel of God's grace."	Acts 20:24
"Now I commit you to God and to the word of his grace, which can build you up and give you an inheritance among all those who are sanctified."	Acts 20:32
". . . justified freely by his grace through the redemption that came by Christ Jesus."	Rom. 3:24
"Therefore, the promise comes by faith, so that it may be by grace and may be guaranteed to all Abraham's offspring."	Rom. 4:16
"How much more will those who receive God's abundant provision of grace and of the gift of righteousness reign in life through the one man, Jesus Christ."	Rom. 5:17
"For sin shall not be your master, because you are not under law, but under grace."	Rom. 6:14
"There is a remnant chosen by grace. And if by grace, then it is no longer by works; if it were, grace would no longer be grace."	Rom. 11:5–6
"We have different gifts, according to the grace given us."	Rom. 12:6

TABLE 27 (*continued*)

Excerpt	Reference
"By the grace God has given me, I laid a foundation."	I Cor. 3:10
"By the grace of God I am what I am, and his grace to me was not without effect. . . . I worked harder than all of them—yet not I, but the grace of God that was with me."	I Cor. 15:10
"We have done so not according to worldly wisdom but according to God's grace."	2 Cor. 1:12
"See that you also excel in this grace of giving."	2 Cor. 8:7
"For you know the grace of our Lord Jesus Christ, that though he was rich, yet for your sakes he became poor."	2 Cor. 8:9
"But he [God] said to me, 'My grace is sufficient for you, for my power is made perfect in weakness.' "	2 Cor. 12:9
"In him we have redemption through his blood, the forgiveness of sins, in accordance with the riches of God's grace that he lavished on us with all wisdom and understanding."	Eph. 1:7
". . . the incomparable riches of his grace, expressed in his kindness to us in Christ Jesus."	Eph. 2:7
"For it is by grace you have been saved, through faith—and this not from yourselves, it is the gift of God—not by works, so that no one can boast."	Eph. 2:8
"Let your conversation be always full of grace, seasoned with salt, so that you may know how to answer everyone."	Col. 4:6
"The grace of our Lord was poured out on me abundantly, along with the faith and love that are in Christ Jesus."	I Tim. 1:14
". . . having been justified by his grace, we might become heirs having the hope of eternal life."	Titus 3:7
"Let us then approach the throne of grace with confidence, so that we may receive mercy and find grace to help us in our time of need."	Heb. 4:16
"But grow in the grace and knowledge of our Lord and Savior Jesus Christ."	2 Peter 3:18

nal presumptions of being in the favour of God, and estate of salvation (which hope of theirs shall perish): yet such as truly believe in the Lord Jesus, and love Him in sincerity, endeavouring to walk in all good conscience before Him, may, in this life, be certainly assured that they are in the state of grace and may rejoice in the hope of the glory of God, which hope shall never make them ashamed.[12]

REDEEMING GRACE UNKNOWN

Redeeming grace is a foreign concept to Islam. It is nowhere mentioned in the Noble Qur'an, nor is it discussed by Islamic scholars. This is a curious thing, given its prominence within the "previous Scriptures."

The truth is that Muhammad knew nothing about grace. Allah is not a gracious god and does not sit on a throne of grace. Allah does not pour grace out upon man to assist him in his struggle. Man must strive alone. Only Qur'anic reminders and submission to Hadithic law are offered to bring him into what he hopes is a state of favor. But this is not the same as a state of grace.

The state of redeeming grace is a liberating position. It frees men to think clear thoughts, study intently, and participate in the progress of human earthly life, all to the glory of the biblical Triune God. Grace encourages people of faith to increase their knowledge about God's creation in order to develop true wisdom in all things.

GRACE AND HUMAN PROGRESS

Islam: A Global Civilization goes to great lengths to convince readers that Muslims were responsible for a multitude of historical discoveries in science and mathematics. But careful reading reveals that much of this work was built on principles originating with the Greeks, and guarded and protected by Christians during the Dark Ages when barbarian hordes swept across Europe. In the book *The Soul of Sci-*

ence, by Nancy R. Pearcey and Charles B. Thaxton, contemporary scientific methodology is described as an outgrowth of the biblical Christian worldview:

It should not be terribly surprising that Christianity was an important ally of the scientific enterprise. After all, modern science arose within a culture saturated with Christian faith. That historical fact alone is suggestive. It was Christianized Europe that became the birthplace of modern science—there and nowhere else.

Through sheer practical know-how and rules-of-thumb, several cultures in antiquity—from the Chinese to the Arabs—produced a higher level of learning and technology than medieval Europe did. Yet it was Christianized Europe and not these more advanced cultures that gave birth to modern science as a systematic, self-correcting discipline.[13]

The biblical Christianity arising out of the Protestant Reformation provided the worldview that "de-deified" creation, permitting men to study it in detail. This had not been encouraged under the rigid theocracy of Roman Catholicism, in the superstitious environment of medieval Europe, or under the pantheistic animism of the pagan Mediterranean region.

This trend continues to the present day. In *Life Alert,* Dr. Korkut notes:

Studies that examine the criteria for the good life for mankind, such as peaceable societies, education, medical care, etc., demonstrate that the Islamic nations are at the bottom of the pile.

145

Scientists of Protestant background have received almost twice as many Nobel prizes as those from all other religious backgrounds combined.[14]

So what does all this have to do with grace? Well, simply put, grace provides the "wind beneath the wings" of all Christian endeavor. Without it, we stay earthbound. With it, we can soar.

Islamic law is mired in the past and will remain so without the illumination of the Spirit of Christ and the outpouring of his grace. Any effort to promote true change, progress, and personal righteousness through seventh-century Islamic law rather than through biblical grace will always fail. As Paul wrote to the Colossians and to the Romans:

> Since you died with Christ to the basic principles of this world, why, as though you still belonged to it, do you submit to its rules: "Do not handle! Do not taste! Do not touch!"? These are all destined to perish with use, because they are based on human commands and teachings. Such regulations indeed have an appearance of wisdom, with their self-imposed worship, their false humility and their harsh treatment of the body, but they lack any value in restraining sensual indulgence. (Col. 2:20–23)

> For you did not receive a spirit that makes you a slave again to fear, but you received the Spirit of sonship. And by him we cry, "*Abba,* Father." (Rom. 8:15)

This is the inheritance of the children of the biblical God. It is vastly more precious and effective than any law imposed by Allah.

GRACE AND DEMOCRACY

Democratic self-government is successful only if citizens demonstrate personal self-government. Through grace men are enabled to make righteous decisions, fulfill earthly responsibilities, enjoy the fruits of their labors, and entertain hope for the future.

Grace in action permits cultures to flourish. Nations that enjoy economic prosperity, political autonomy, and intellectual strength are those in which individuals have the greatest freedom to fully participate in their culture. People are trusted to use their gifts wisely and encouraged to make positive contributions.

American history has much to teach us regarding the importance of biblical Christianity in the establishment of American democracy, although its role has been downplayed by historical revisionists over the last century. But fortunately, original source documents remain unchanged, and a survey of their content is quite revealing. What follows is a group of quotations demonstrating biblical Christianity's influence on the American republic:

BIBLICAL CHRISTIANITY AND THE FOUNDING OF THE AMERICAN REPUBLIC

"The God who gave us life gave us liberty at the same time. . . . The last hope of human liberty in this world rests on us." —Thomas Jefferson

"We have staked the whole future civilization, not upon the power of government, far from it. We have staked the future of all of our political institutions upon the capacity of each and all of us to govern ourselves, to control ourselves, to sustain ourselves according to the Ten Commandments of God." —James Madison

"No people can be bound to acknowledge and adore the invisible hand which conducts the affairs of men more than the people of the United States. Every step by which they have advanced to the character of an independent nation seems to have been distinguished by some token of Providential agency. . . . We ought to be no less persuaded that the propitious smiles of heaven can not be expected on a nation that disregards the eternal rules of order and right, which heaven itself has ordained." —Benjamin Franklin

"We have had a hard struggle, but the Almighty has favored the just cause; and I join most heartily with you in your prayers that he may perfect his work and establish freedom in the new world as an asylum for those of the old, who deserve it." —Benjamin Franklin

"The promulgation of the great doctrines of religion, the being, and attributes, and providence of one Almighty God; the responsibility to him for all our actions, founded upon moral freedom and accountability; a future state of rewards and punishments; the cultivation of all the personal, social, and benevolent virtues—these can never be matters of indifference in any well-ordered community. It is, indeed, difficult to conceive how any civilized society can exist without them." —Joseph Story

"To the Pulpit, the Puritan Pulpit, we owe the moral force which won our Independence." —John Wingate Thornton

"The only foundation for a useful education in a republic is to be laid in religion. Without it there can be no virtue, and without virtue there can be no liberty, and liberty is the object and life of all republican governments." —Dr. Benjamin Rush

"A Christian, I say again, cannot fail of being a republican, for every precept of the Gospel inculcates those degrees of humility, self-denial, and brotherly kindness, which are directly opposed to the pride of monarchy and the pageantry of a court." —Dr. Benjamin Rush

"The Bible contains the most profound philosophy, the most perfect morality, and the most refined policy, that ever was conceived upon earth. It is the most republican book in the world." —John Adams

"The Christian religion ought to be received and maintained with firm and cordial support. It is the real source of all genuine republican principles. It teaches the equality of men as to rights and duties; and while it forbids all oppression, it commands due subordination to law and rulers. It requires the young to yield obedience to their parents, and enjoins upon men the duty of selecting their rulers from their fellow citizens of mature age, sound wisdom, and real religion." —Noah Webster

"Those who destroy the influence and authority of the Christian religion, sap the foundations of public

order, of liberty, and of republican government."
—Noah Webster

"As piety and virtue support the honour and happiness of every community, they are peculiarly required in a free government. Virtue is the spirit of a republic; for where all power is derived from the people, all depends on their good disposition." —Dr. Samuel Cooper

"Freedom sees religion as the companion of its struggles and triumphs, the cradle of its infancy, and the divine source of its rights. Religion is considered as the guardian of mores, and mores are regarded as the guarantee of the laws and pledge for the maintenance of freedom itself." —Alexis de Tocqueville

"We hold these truths to be self-evident, that all men are created equal, that they are endowed by their Creator with certain unalienable rights, that among these are Life, Liberty and the pursuit of Happiness." —The Declaration of Independence

"It would be peculiarly improper to omit, in this first official act, my fervent supplications to that Almighty Being who rules over the universe, who presides in the councils of nations, and whose providential aids can supply every human defect, that His benediction may consecrate to the liberties and happiness of the people of the United States." —George Washington, First Inaugural Address

"For the Americans the ideas of Christianity and liberty are so completely mingled that it is almost impossible to get them to conceive of the one without the other." —Alexis de Tocqueville

"O! thus be it ever when free men shall stand
Between their loved home and the war's desolation;
Blest with vict'ry and peace, may the Heav'n-
    rescued land
Praise the Pow'r that hath made and preserved us
    a nation!
Then conquer we must, when our cause it is just;
And this be our motto, 'In God is our trust!'
And the star-spangled banner in triumph shall wave
O'er the land of the free and the home of the brave!"
—Final stanza of the United States National Anthem

IS ISLAMIC DEMOCRACY POSSIBLE?

Islamic democracy is an oxymoron. No nation embracing Muslim shari'ah has ever been a democratic republic. Dictatorship has always been the norm in Islamic countries. Absolute power rests in the hands of a single despot or family, supported by religious authorities and military might. Shari'ah law is applied rigorously, basic human rights are abrogated, and civil liberties are curtailed. "The history of the Islamic states is 'one of almost unrelieved autocracy. The Muslim subject owed obedience to a legitimate Muslim ruler as a religious duty. That is to say, disobedience was a sin as well as a crime.' "[15]

Today's international community tries to put the cart before the horse when it encourages democratic reform in Islamic nations. It does not realize that Muslim doctrine denies the very notion of personal liberties and is completely incompatible with the idea of participatory government or

151

representative law. Again, most Muslims already know this. As King Fahd of Saudi Arabia freely admitted: "The Democratic system that is predominant in the world is not a suitable system for the peoples of our region. . . . The system of free elections is not suitable to our country."[16] He is, of course, absolutely right. "Democracy depends on freedom of thought and free discussion, whereas Islamic law explicitly forbids the discussions of decisions arrived at by the infallible consensus of the ulama."[17]

Throughout the history of Islam, the essential components of democratic systems such as representative assemblies, legislative institutions, and legal jurisprudence have been unknown. Unlike the Puritans, Quakers, Congregationalists, and other Christian freedom-seekers who established communities in colonial America, the Muslim people are in many ways totally unprepared for the responsibilities of self-government.

This phenomenon can be traced back to the very foundational beliefs regarding God, man, and the nature of their relationship. The biblical Christianity that reemerged during the Reformation provided the practical theological framework that nurtured the development of democratic ideology. Conversely, the practical theology of Islam retards such development.

Is Islamic democracy possible? "The truth of the matter is that Islam will never achieve democracy and human rights if it insists on the application of the sharia."[18]

ISLAMIC DA'WAH

Islam does not want democracy for itself, but it does desire to exploit its freedoms in order to introduce shari'ah. On the Web site islaam.com, an article entitled "Priorities of Islamic Activities in the West," attributed to Shaykh 'Abdul Rahman 'Abdul Khaliq, recently appeared. The following is a brief summary of its contents (italics ours):

1. Muslims must re-establish unity in this nation all over the world. They must be loyal to other Muslims and *disloyal to all Kuffar [non-Muslims]*.
2. Muslims must affirm the basic belief that *Muslims are members of the best nation ever that was introduced to humanity*. The struggle between Islam and Christianity will last till the end of time. Muslims must also preserve the Islamic code of dress, eat Islamic foods, and marry Muslim women and, if they wish, only pure and good Christian women.
3. *Arabic must be the first language for all Muslims again.*
4. Muslims must perform *Da'wah (propagate Islam) wherever they may be.*
5. Muslims should warn of all misguided groups and define the one righteous group. *To fight against misguided groups and off-shoot sects is a necessity.*
6. Muslims of the West must be united in every matter. They must call to Islam and preserve their loyalty to Muslims and *be disloyal to the disbelievers.*
7. Muslims must *establish Islamic schools* that will preserve and teach Islam to their children in their first years.
8. Muslims everywhere must seek to *protect the religious, educational, and social rights of Muslim minorities* in the West. Muslims of the West *must not be prevented from practicing and propagating Islam, the true religion.*

153

9. A higher authority for the benefit of Muslim immigrants must be established to *protect the rights of Muslim minorities.*

10. Muslims must establish committees composed of Muslim scholars that will teach the religion to Muslim immigrants and *solve their problems according to the Qur'an and the Sunnah.*

11. Muslims must *establish a sound economic system* that will benefit Muslim immigrants in the West.

This represents an aggressive agenda for the intense propagation of Islam in America, drawn from the clear historical pattern of Muslim expansionism around the world. It is a political-action manifesto targeted at the exploitation of the freedoms of democracy in order to ultimately establish its antithesis—subjugation to Islamic shari'ah law.

The Noble Qur'an is not subtle about its disregard for people of other faiths. It is no secret that the freedoms and rights demanded by Muslims as quoted above are denied to other religions in all Islamic countries. Table 28 presents suras that address Islam's inherent militancy toward all other belief systems.

THE CHRISTIAN RESPONSE

This militancy demands a response, but not the one you might think. The Christian attitude must always be one that reflects Jesus Christ, who commanded us to love our enemies. This requires great compassion and commitment—as well as a great deal of grace.

Biblical Christians must recognize the need for outreach to the Muslim community and commit themselves to it.

Although Islam discourages Muslim interaction with Christians, Christians must take the initiative, as Yahweh has done for us, and not allow this separation to succeed.

Qur'anic Islam needs what biblical Christianity has. Muslims are under bondage—to law, to fear, to hatred. This

TABLE 28   Sample militant passages in the Noble Qur'an

Excerpt	Sura
"Soon shall We cast terror into the hearts of the Unbelievers, for that they joined companions with Allah, for which He had sent no authority: their abode will be the Fire; and evil is the home of the wrong-doers!"	3:151
"Let those fight in the cause of Allah who sell the life of this world for the Hereafter. To him who fights in the cause of Allah,—whether he is slain or gets victory—soon shall We give him a reward of great (value)."	4:74
"And those who reject Faith fight in the cause of Evil: so fight against the Friends of Satan."	4:76
"For the Unbelievers are open enemies unto you."	4:101
"And do not slacken in following up the enemy ."	4:104
"O ye who believe! take not the Jews and the Christians for your friends and protectors."	5:51
"How many towns have We destroyed (for their sins)? Our punishment took them on a sudden by night or while they slept for their afternoon rest."	7:4
"O Messenger! rouse the Believers to the fight. If there are twenty amongst you, patient and persevering, they will vanquish two hundred: if a hundred, they will vanquish a thousand of the Unbelievers: for these are a people without understanding."	8:65
"It is not fitting for a Messenger that he should have prisoners of war until He has thoroughly subdued the land."	8:67
"Fight those who do not believe in Allah nor the Last Day, . . . nor acknowledge the Religion of Truth, (even if they are) of the People of the Book, until they pay the Jizya [tax] with willing submission, and feel themselves subdued."	9:29
"O you who believe! Fight the Unbelievers who gird you about, and let them find firmness in you."	9:123
"Therefore, when ye meet the Unbelievers (in fight), smite at their necks; at length, when ye have thoroughly subdued then, bind a bond firmly (on them)."	47:4

bondage is not due to the rejection of God, but rather to something even more frightening: submission to a distorted and false concept of God. Freedom from this bondage is not found in religion about God, but in relationship with the real, living, active biblical Triune God, through his Son, Jesus Christ. And relationships cannot be forced; they must be nurtured.

So it is with our Muslim neighbors, across the street or around the world. Their emancipation must be achieved face to face and one soul at a time. Writes Christine A. Mallouhi in her book *Waging Peace on Islam:*

> Muslims need to see Jesus and the only way most of them will see him is in us. Muslims are still waiting for Christians who will cross the battle lines to meet them in the spirit of Jesus. And what about those Muslims who see us as the enemy? There is only one Biblical way to deal with enemies—out-love their enmity.[19]

Table 29 describes a *radical pacifism* that is totally impossible without the grace of God. Clearly, it is beyond human nature to rest so securely in his love and power, and resist the fleshly response to initiate conflict in the name of God, exact revenge, or aggressively assert ourselves over others. Only the active grace bestowed by Jesus Christ can enable men to respond to one another with such divine compassion.

"THE SAVIOUR"

Thou God of all grace,
Thou hast given me a saviour,
produce in me a faith to live by him,
    to make him all my desire,

TABLE 29   Sample passages on godly attitudes in the Holy Bible

Excerpt	Reference
"Blessed are the peacemakers, for they will be called sons of God."	Matt. 5:9
"Blessed are you when people insult you, persecute you and falsely say all kinds of evil against you because of me."	Matt. 5:11
"But I tell you, Do not resist an evil person. If someone strikes you on the right cheek, turn to him the other also."	Matt. 5:39
"You have heard that it was said, 'Love your neighbor and hate your enemy.' But I tell you: Love your enemies and pray for those who persecute you, that you may be sons of your Father in heaven."	Matt. 5:43–45
"For if you forgive men when they sin against you, your heavenly Father will also forgive you."	Matt. 6:14
"Bless those who persecute you; bless and do not curse."	Rom. 12:14
"Do not repay anyone evil for evil. . . . Do not take revenge. . . . overcome evil with good."	Rom. 12:17, 19, 21
"For though we live in the world, we do not wage war as the world does. The weapons we fight with are not the weapons of the world."	2 Cor. 10:3–4
"Get rid of all bitterness, rage and anger, brawling and slander, along with every form of malice. Be kind and compassionate to one another, forgiving each other, just as in Christ God forgave you."	Eph. 4:31–32
"Clothe yourselves with compassion, kindness, humility, gentleness and patience. Bear with each other and forgive whatever grievances you may have against one another. Forgive as the Lord forgave you."	Col. 3:12–13
"Make sure that nobody pays back wrong for wrong, but always try to be kind to each other and to everyone else."	1 Thess. 5:15
" 'Put your sword back in its place,' Jesus said to him, 'for all who draw the sword will die by the sword.' "	Matt. 26:52

all my hope,
all my glory.
May I enter him as my refuge,
    build on him as my foundation,
    walk in him as my way,
    follow him as my guide,
    conform to him as my example,

receive his instructions as my prophet,
rely on his intercession as my high priest,
obey him as my king.
May I never be ashamed of him or his words,
but joyfully bear his reproach,
never displease him by unholy or imprudent
conduct,
never count it a glory if I take it patiently
when buffeted for a fault,
never make the multitude my model,
never delay when thy Word invites me to
advance.
May thy dear Son preserve me from this present evi
world,
so that its smiles never allure,
nor its frowns terrify,
nor its vices defile,
nor its errors delude me.
May I feel that I am a stranger and a pilgrim on
earth,
declaring plainly that I seek a country,
my title to it becoming daily more clear,
my meetness for it more perfect,
my foretastes of it more abundant;
and whatsoever I do may it be done in the
Saviour's name.[20]

7

COMMUNICATING
THE GOSPEL OF GRACE
TO MUSLIMS

As we have seen, communication depends on the transmission of meaning from one mind to another. We can do this in a variety of ways, verbal and nonverbal. But we have also seen that similar words, gestures, or postures do not necessarily convey similar meanings to different audiences and must be clarified before they can be fully understood.

God's mind has transmitted the meaning of divine love and salvation through his Scripture and his Son. He has communicated with us in word and deed, and the meaning of Divine Truth has been translated and demonstrated to all, making his plan absolutely clear and his Person known. He knows that his message is too important to be left to chance or misunderstanding.

OUR MISSION—COMMUNICATION

The biblical Triune God has commanded that Christians tell others about his marvelous grace and the good news of the gospel of reconciliation. Believers in Jesus have been commissioned by the Lord to communicate his great message to all mankind. Biblical Christians are all missionaries.

But how is this mission work effectively carried out? There is no one-size-fits-all method of presenting or bringing the gospel to others. Although step-by-step evangelism guides abound, providing useful tools for the committed Christian, there is simply no substitute for the development of real, honest, and trusting relationships. Remember, the Triune God is a relational God, and Christians must be relational people as we follow him.

As we seek to confront Muslims with Jesus Christ, we must rely upon the dynamic fascination of radiant, Christlike living. It is more subtle than reasoned argument, more persuasive than an educational enterprise, and more effective than any amount of formal religious instruction.[1]

JESUS: THE MASTER MISSIONARY

Turning to the Holy Bible, which is always our source for Truth in all things, we find many incidents demonstrating the way in which Jesus, the Master Missionary, communicated with others. We will look specifically at two models.

The first is taken from John 4:4–30. In this passage, Jesus was traveling through Samaria on his way to Galilee. Jews usually avoided Samaritan areas for fear of being attacked.

Reading through the passage, we can develop the following outline of this encounter:

160

1. Jesus makes a humble request for a drink. He directs his request to a Samaritan woman. It is important to realize that not only is it remarkable that he, a Jew, should appeal to a Samaritan, but it is truly astounding that he should speak publicly to a woman—any woman! He breaks the social rules here, and it is duly noted by the woman he addresses.

2. He draws an analogy between his need for "earthly" water and her need for "living" water. Although she does not understand his reference at first, it intrigues her and causes her to ask him for the living water he offers.

3. He describes something about her private life that immediately reveals his status as a prophet. Her response is to engage him in theological discussion regarding places of worship, a sore spot in Samaritan-Jewish relations.

   Jesus is not reluctant to enter into this type of discussion. In fact, the dialogue in this passage is one of the longest sustained conversations recorded in the New Testament. He is eager to share his perfect knowledge and understanding with her.

   Consequently, he honors her desire for clarification and information and reveals deep truth to her regarding the proper worship of God and his nature. In response, she confesses her belief in the Messiah.

4. He proclaims his identity as the Christ. Her response is to go immediately and tell others, testifying about her conversation with Jesus, and urging them to come to him.

The result: The Samaritan woman becomes one of the first missionaries!

Learning from the John 4 Model. There are four points to be gleaned from this encounter:

- Take the initiative in humble outreach to anyone in need.
- Make connections between the earthly life of the hearer and the spiritual life offered in Christ.
- Give clear and gentle instruction regarding foundational truths.
- Boldly proclaim the Person of Christ.

JESUS: RESURRECTED MISSIONARY

The second model we will look at is that in Luke 24:13–32. An incognito Jesus joins two travelers as they are returning from Jerusalem after his resurrection. The travelers have been among the disciples, and they relate to Jesus their testimony regarding the resurrection. Their encounter with the risen Christ follows this pattern:

1. Jesus walks with them and listens attentively to their recounting of the events surrounding his own death and resurrection.
2. He uses the Scriptures and the Prophets to illuminate the meaning of the events for them.
3. He accepts their invitation to break bread with them, blessing the bread and offering it to the others.
4. They are given the gift of recognition and see him for who he really is. Only then do they reflect on the

emotional impact of his presence as he explained and expounded the Word to them on the road.

Learning from the Luke 24 Model. The following points are illuminated in this model:

- Walk with others and listen, listen, listen.
- Ask questions and use the Holy Bible to instruct.
- Enjoy fellowship, hospitality, and breaking bread with other Truth-seekers.
- Pray that others may receive the gift of eye-opening recognition and see Christ Jesus as he really is!

THE APOSTLES: STUDENTS OF THE MASTER

Our next model comes from the event recounted in Acts 2:1–41. It is Pentecost, and the disciples are blessed with the anointing of the Holy Spirit. This enables them to speak and to be understood by people from many different geographic and linguistic areas, allowing them to give testimony of Christ to all nations and tribes at the same time.

The speech given by Peter is recorded in verses 14–36. It follows this pattern:

1. Peter corrects the misperceptions of the disciples' remarkable behavior and explains it in terms of scriptural fulfillment, quoting the prophet Joel.
2. He reaffirms the historical truth already known about Jesus Christ.
3. He gives testimony regarding the resurrection and confirms the event with Old Testament prophecy.

4. He frames current events in terms of biblical prophecy and clearly proclaims Jesus as the Christ.

In response, the hearts of those who hear Peter are seized with the recognition of their own sinfulness and their need for salvation. They plead with Peter to tell them what to do, to which he replies, "Repent and be baptized in the name of Jesus Christ."

Learning from the Acts 2 Model

- Use the Holy Scriptures to gently correct misconceptions.
- Reaffirm the truths that listeners may already know about Christ.
- Confirm the resurrection truth with personal and biblical testimony.
- Reinterpret current situations in terms of timeless biblical principles.

PAUL'S MODEL IN ACTS 17

This event is thoroughly explored in Dr. Bahnsen's book *Always Ready.* The apostle Paul addresses the scholars and philosophers at the Areopagus in Athens with a sermon designed to touch the hearts of those mired in pantheism and misguided worship. His speech is a masterpiece of Christian apologetics and gives us a fine paradigm for presenting the gospel in similar circumstances.

1. Paul addresses his listeners directly and respectfully, honoring their desire to know Truth. Notice that he

is careful to commend them without validating their distorted worldview.

2. He highlights the differences between the two antithetical presuppositional positions: pagan polytheism and biblical monotheism.
3. He exposes the inherent deficiencies of the nonbiblical worldview and its suppression of the Truth in the light of the revelatory authority of Scripture.
4. He calls for his hearers' repentance and dependence on Christ, requiring a complete change of mind-set initiated by the Holy Spirit.

It is important to realize that in this apologetic, Paul does not suggest any integration of worldviews or syncretism between pagan musings and revealed Truth. His speech is not designed to propose a "natural theology" that blurs or merges the two positions. Rather, he is firm in clearly defining the sharp differences and using the Holy Scriptures to focus the image of the biblical Triune God for his listeners.

Learning from the Acts 17 Model

- Show honor and respect, without giving the impression of agreement with false presuppositions.
- Use the Scriptures to highlight the shortcomings of the nonbiblical position.
- Be bold to proclaim Christ and call for repentance.

THE PRESUPPOSITIONAL MODEL

In the introduction of this volume, we clearly stated that we would present the information from the presuppositional position that Divine Truth was fully contained in the Holy Bible, uncorrupted and trustworthy. This is the primary foundational position reflected in all the previous models of biblical missionary communication.

Other common characteristics of these models include the following:

- Fostering mutual respect between Christian and non-Christian, including careful and attentive listening to one another, taking the initiative to reach out in compassion, and taking the time to form relationships.
- Allowing biblical spiritual insight to anoint the relationship, balancing boldness and sensitivity through the leading of the Holy Spirit.
- Using the Holy Scriptures as the primary source of gentle instruction and humble appeal, without compromising Truth in order to build bridges, but instead using Truth as the bridge.
- Presenting Jesus Christ to others in both word and deed and praying continually that his voice and Person may be recognized.
- Boldly proclaiming him and inviting repentance in his name.

A MISSION OF JOY

Finally, those who desire to communicate Christ to others must see "mission" in a new light. It is an honor and a delight to be called as an adopted child of Yahweh, and sharing this privilege with others should be the Christian's greatest joy. Therefore, mission should be seen as:

- Celebration of our intimacy with God.
- Proclamation of the timeless and unaltered message of Truth.
- Interpretation of the message to impact the lives of others.
- Reconciliation of the lost to their Heavenly Father. Animosity is transformed into fellowship, friendship, and, ultimately, "family" membership.
- Incarnation of Christlikeness in other Truth-seekers.

BUILDING A "CHURCH WITHOUT WALLS"

Church Without Walls (CWW), a ministry of the Presbyterian Church in America, has been actively engaged in this effort for 22 years, with the following goals:

1. To communicate the gospel of Jesus Christ's redemption and love to Muslims in North America.
2. To help Muslims understand the biblical faith.
3. To help Muslims receive God's gift of life in Jesus Christ, the promised Messiah and the Eternal Son of the Father.
4. To help nurture and disciple those who are saved and to encourage each one to join wholeheartedly in a PCA or other Bible-believing fellowship.

This outreach model is called "Meetings for Better Understanding" and is fashioned as a format for truthful conversation between Muslims and Christians on a variety of theological topics. Passages from the Noble Qur'an and the Holy Bible are read aloud and speakers are given equal and ample time to explain and expound upon the readings, focusing respectful and honest discussion on a previously agreed-upon topic. It is being successfully used across America and in some overseas locations.

CWW emphasizes that in order for these groups to reach out to one another effectively, several barriers to free communication must come down:

The Wall of Hatred. Sadly, Christians and Muslims do not see each other as human beings created in the image of God. Harsh treatment and rhetoric about one another has fueled the feeling of enmity.

The Wall of Distrust. Relationships between Christians and Muslims have often been reduced to false accusations, fiery debates, and uncivilized behavior. They have both been poor examples of their respective faiths.

The Wall of Isolation. Communities of Christians and Muslims turn inward and do not associate with one another. Isolation always leads to alienation.

The Wall of Misunderstanding. Rumors and misinformation about both faiths is rampant. Neither group has read the other's sacred literature or explored historical or contemporary commentary.

The Wall of Miscommunication. The four previous walls have adversely affected the process of exchanging reliable information between Muslim and Christian communities. Clarity of dialogue and thoughtful definition of terminology is therefore of utmost importance. So, too, is complete and truthful exposition of sacred texts and principles.

The Wall of Conversion. Men do not convert other men. God converts men. Adherents of either faith should not enter relationships with one another for the sole purpose of making converts. The first goal is better understanding. The Holy Spirit is in charge of the rest.

To remove these walls, CWW recommends the following principles:

- Learn to listen to one another and listen to learn about one another.
- Overcome stereotypes and see people clearly.
- Understand and clarify that Western culture is *not* biblical Christianity!
- Contextualize the message.
- Adapt cross-culturally when biblically permissible.
- Plow and sow for the Kingdom.
- Be prepared to discuss the Holy Trinity. It is a main source of misunderstanding and error for Muslims.
- Be sensitive to secret Christians among the Muslims.
- Practice Christian community and genuine brotherly love.

Table 30 summarizes a few basic guidelines for Christians when developing relationships with Muslims. Christians involved in Meetings for Better Understanding will find their task lightened if certain other conditions are met. Before the meeting, prayer, fasting, and careful Bible study are recommended for spiritual preparation.

The Holy Bible and Noble Qur'an must serve as the source documents for the discussion. Both books should be open and available as the conversation progresses. Muslims need

TABLE 30 Guidelines for Christians in Muslim-Christian relationships

Dos	Don'ts
Pray for the guidance and protection of the Holy Spirit before each meeting.	Don't be confrontational or easily provoked to anger.
Be relational. Ask about nonreligious personal things first. Establish a nonthreatening rapport.	Don't have a patronizing attitude or tell Muslims what they believe.
Listen intently while Muslims talk.	Don't put your Bible on the floor or place other objects on top of it.
Be respectful when they voice their beliefs.	Don't feel that you have to answer all their questions right away.
Affirm what you can about their beliefs. There are some points of intersection!	Don't engage in long one-on-one conversations with someone of the opposite sex.
Be willing to read Islamic materials and attend Muslim functions.	Don't offer to shake hands with Muslims of the opposite sex.
Be sincere. People are not "spiritual projects."	Don't dress inappropriately. Modesty is the rule.
Share Christ by using Scripture and personal testimony.	Don't be argumentative in proclaiming and defending the biblical faith.
Take the initiative in suggesting another meeting.	Don't offer Muslims pork or alcohol.

to hear, read, and understand the Holy Bible and must be given ample time to read the biblical references for themselves as they are cited. The Bible as the Word of God has its own authority and power and should be the heart of the conversation. Continual prayer should be offered that Yahweh will speak through his Word. We must earnestly ask the Holy Spirit to guide all participants to find the Truth.

Christians must be prepared to explain the context of the quoted biblical passages. This will assist Muslims in seeing the whole picture. Christians should avoid quoting controversial theologians whose ideas are not in agreement with orthodox, historical biblical Christianity. Conversely, Muslims are encouraged to avoid Qur'anic scholars who are not in agreement with accepted Islamic thought.

If these conditions are followed, basic civil conduct will be more likely to result. There is no place for militant Muslim or Christian behavior in these meetings. Although each person has the basic human right to express himself and his beliefs with full freedom of thought and liberty of expression, this right is not a license to denigrate one another. Therefore, anger and rudeness are not tolerated, and one may not interrupt another or display disrespect orally or otherwise.

This civility is in keeping with both biblical and Qur'anic precepts:

> Invite (all) to the Way of thy Lord with wisdom and beautiful preaching: and argue with them in ways that are best and most gracious. (Sura 16:125)

> A word aptly spoken is like apples of gold in settings of silver. (Prov. 25:11)

FOUR IDEOLOGICAL POSITIONS

During the conversation, four distinct types of positions will be expressed concerning Qur'anic Islam and biblical Christian doctrines. It is important to know and understand these positions in order to navigate through them during the discussion. Table 31 lists and defines them.

Samuel M. Zwemer, in his book *The Muslim Christ,* offers the following:

> We must become Moslems to the Moslem if we would gain them for Christ. We must do this in the Pauline

171

TABLE 31   Ideological positions

Position	Definition
Conflict	Beliefs are fundamentally irreconcilable.
Contrast	From a liberal viewpoint, no "genuine" conflict exists since Muslims and Christians are responding to radically different questions concerning their beliefs, which really "do not differ."
Contact	Better understanding, amicable interaction, and ways to find "common ground" in shaping religious thought are possible.
Confirmation	Highlight the ways Muslims and Christians support and nourish their entire religious conversation on a very deep and personal level, motivating each to seek Truth in the Person of God himself.

sense, without compromise, but with self-sacrificing sympathy and unselfish love.

The nearest way to the Moslem heart can often be found better by subjective than by objective study. The barrier may be in the heart of the missionary as well as in the heart of the Moslem. He should cultivate sympathy to the highest degree and an appreciation of all the great fundamental truths which we hold in common with Moslems. He should show the superiority of Christianity both in doctrine and life by admitting the excellences of doctrine and life in [Islam], but showing immediately how Christianity far surpasses them.

The heart of the Gospel and that which possesses the greatest power of appeal to [Muslims], as to every sinner, is the union between God's mercy and God's justice manifested in the Cross of Christ. When properly presented, this doctrine is not only absolutely noble but compelling to any [Muslim] who feels a sense of sin. In order to awaken a sense of sin, which is essential in all missionary effort, the ethical standards of the Sermon on the Mount and the spotless purity of the life of Christ must be presented.

We should ask every sincere Moslem inquirer to study the Gospel story and try for himself to reach a true estimate of Jesus Christ, of whom Mohammed spoke in such high terms of honour as a Prophet and an Apostle of God; to take the historical foundations of the Christian religion and examine them as critically as he pleases, and to see for himself what Jesus claimed to be, and how His claims were understood by His disciples and by the early Church.

In other words, we should press home the question Jesus Himself put to His disciples and to the world, "What think ye of the Christ?"[2]

Most biblical Christians are intimidated by the militancy of Islam, but it need not be so. Indeed, says Fuoad Masri in his article "Muslim Extremists and the Great Commission": "Islamic extremism is living proof that Muslims are searching for God. They are in need of a deep relationship with a living savior."[3]

Again, Samuel Zwemer gives us an example of this internal deep longing among Muslims. The following is a Sufi prayer:

I am truly bankrupt, O God. I stand before the door of thy riches. Truly I have great sins—forgive me for Thine own sake. Truly I am a stranger, a sinner, a humble slave who has nothing but forgetfulness and disobedience to present to Thee. My sins are as the sands, without number. Forgive me and pardon me. Remove my transgressions and undertake my cause. Truly my

173

heart is sick, but Thou art able to heal it. My condition, O God, is such that I have no good work. My evil deeds are many, and my provision of obedience is small. Speak to the fire of my heart, as Thou didst in the case of Abraham, "be cool for my servant."[4]

Zwemer asks at the end of this passage, "What do you make of such prayers of pardon?" It is the cry of sheep without a shepherd. This plea should motivate every Christian to seek the hungering Muslim who is lost and bring him unto the fold, where the safety and rest of Jesus awaits him.

In the words of Paul to the Romans:

Brothers, my heart's desire and prayer to God for the Israelites [or Muslims] is that they may be saved. For I can testify about them that they are zealous for God, but their zeal is not based on knowledge. Since they did not know the righteousness that comes from God and sought to establish their own, they did not submit to God's righteousness. Christ is the end of the law so that there may be righteousness for everyone who believes. (Rom. 10:1–4)

With that same heart's desire we commit this work to the Holy Spirit. If you are a Muslim and have read this book with an open heart and mind, we commend your desire to know Truth. If the Spirit of the living God is speaking to you, calling you to himself in Christ Jesus, we invite you to offer the following prayer of repentance and acceptance:

Dear Lord Jesus, I know that I am a sinner and need your forgiveness. I believe that you died for my sins and that I can come into the presence of God

Almighty only through your perfect life and sacrifice, clothed in your righteousness alone. You have called me to be your child, and I ask you to cleanse me and make me your own. Thank you for this free gift of your grace and the promise of life eternal with you. In your Holy Name, Amen.

"COME TO THE WATERS"

Come to the waters, whoever is thirsty;
Drink from the Fountain that never runs dry.
Jesus, the Living One, offers you mercy,
Life more abundant in boundless supply.

Come to the River that flows through the city,
Forth from the throne of the Father and Son.
Jesus the Savior says, "Come and drink deeply."
Drink from the pure, inexhaustible One.

Come to the Fountain without any money;
Buy what is given without any cost.
Jesus, the gracious One, welcomes the weary;
Jesus, the selfless One, died for the lost.

Come to the Well of unmerited favor;
Stretch out your hand; fill your cup to the brim.
Jesus is such a compassionate Savior.
Draw from the grace that flows freely from him.

Come to the Savior, the God of salvation.
God has provided an end to sin's strife.
Why will you suffer the Law's condemnation?
Take the free gift of the water of life.[5]

175

NOTES

Preface

1. Os Guinness, *Time for Truth: Living Free in a World of Lies, Hype, and Spin* (Grand Rapids: Baker, 2000), 14, italics his.

Introduction

1. Islamic Affairs Department, *Islam: A Global Civilization* (Washington, D.C.: The Embassy of Saudi Arabia, n.d.), 7.

2. Greg L. Bahnsen, *Always Ready: Directions for Defending the Faith* (Nacogdoches, Tex.: Covenant Media Foundation, 1996), 25.

Chapter 1: "Truth" in Qur'anic Islam and Biblical Christianity

1. Charles Crismier, *Renewing the Soul of America* (Richmond, Va.: Elijah, 2002), 88.

2. Ibn Warraq, *Origins of the Koran: Classic Essays on Islam's Holy Book* (Amherst, Mass.: Prometheus, 1998), 97.

3. Ibid., 98.

4. C. S. Lewis, *Mere Christianity* (New York: Simon & Schuster, 1943), 37.

5. Samuel P. Schlorff, "Muslim Ideology and Christian Apologetics," *Missiology: An International Review* 21, no. 2 (1993): 175.

6. Islamic Affairs Department, *Islam: A Global Civilization* (Washington, D.C.: The Embassy of Saudi Arabia, n.d.), 7.

7. Ibid., 9.

8. Ibid.

9. Ibid.

10. Farid Esack, *On Being a Muslim* (Oxford: Oneworld, 1999), 5.

11. Ibid., 10.

12. Thomas Cleary, *The Wisdom of the Prophet: Sayings of Muhammad* (Boston: Shambhala, 1994), 38–39.

13. Ibid., 104.

14. Ibid., 110.

177

15. J. I. Packer, *Knowing God* (Downers Grove, Ill.: InterVarsity Press, 1973), 32.

Chapter 2: The Truth about Muhammad

1. Georges Houssney, "Arabia in the Bible and the Qur'an," *ReachOut* (June 1989): 16.

2. Ibid., 8.

3. Ibn Warraq, *Why I Am Not a Muslim* (Amherst, Mass.: Prometheus, 1995), 89.

4. Ibn Warraq, *Origins of the Koran: Classic Essays on Islam's Holy Book* (Amherst, Mass.: Prometheus, 1998), 25.

5. Norman L. Geisler and Abdul Saleeb, *Answering Islam* (Grand Rapids: Baker, 1993), 163.

6. Ibid., 84

7. Imam an-Nawawi, "Prophet Muhammad's Miracles" (Daar us-Sunnah Publications, 2001), accessed at www.islaam.com/Article.asp?=596, October 22, 2002.

8. Abdul Radhi Muhammad Abdul Mohsen, "The Prophet Muhammad's Conduct and Morals as an Evidence of His Prophethood" (IIPH, 1999), accessed at www.islaam.com/Article.asp?id=424, October 22, 2002.

9. Geisler and Saleeb, *Answering Islam,* 86.

10. James A. Beverly, *Understanding Islam* (Nashville: Thomas Nelson, 2001), 14.

11. Samuel M. Zwemer, *The Muslim Christ* (Edinburgh: Oliphant, Anderson & Ferrier, 1912), 157.

12. Ibid., 157–60.

13. Ibid., 160–61.

14. Quoted in Geisler and Saleeb, *Answering Islam,* 82.

15. Samuel M. Zwemer, *Islam and the Cross* (Phillipsburg, N.J.: P&R Publishing, 2002), 70.

16. Edward J. Young, *My Servants the Prophets* (Grand Rapids: Eerdmans, 1952), 152.

17. Ibid., 145.

18. Ibn Warraq, *The Quest for the Historical Muhammad* (Amherst, Mass.: Prometheus, 2000), 103.

Chapter 3: Jesus Christ in Qur'anic and Biblical Thought

1. "Comparative Religions: Jesus on Whom Be Peace in the Glorious Qur'an" (Toronto: Islamic Information & Da'wah Center International),

accessed at www.islaminfo.com/articleview.asp?level=1&catID=1, October 16, 2002.

2. Abdullah Yusuf Ali, *The Qur'an* (Elmhurst, N.Y.: Tahrike Tarsile Qur'an, 2001), 230.

3. Moishe Rosen, *Y'shua* (Chicago: Moody Press, 1982), 1.

4. Ibid., 10.

5. Samuel M. Zwemer, *The Muslim Christ* (Edinburgh: Oliphant, Anderson & Ferrier, 1912), 35.

6. Ibid., 36.

7. Robert L. Reymond, *Jesus, Divine Messiah* (Phillipsburg, N.J.: P&R Publishing, 1990), 19.

8. Quoted in ibid., 243.

9. "There's Something about That Name," Words by William J. and Gloria Gaither. Music by William J. Gaither. Copyright © 1970 William J. Gaither, Inc. All rights controlled by Gaither Copyright Management. Used by permission.

Chapter 4: The Noble Qur'an and the Holy Bible

1. Islamic Affairs Department, *Islam: A Global Civilization* (Washington, D.C.: The Embassy of Saudi Arabia, n.d.), 7.

2. Abdullah Yusuf Ali, *The Qur'an* (Elmhurst, N.Y.: Tahrike Tarsile Qur'an, 2001), xvi.

3. Michael Sells, *Approaching the Qur'an* (Ashland, Ore.: White Cloud Press, 1999), 4.

4. Ibid., 11.

5. Islamic Affairs Department, *Islam: A Global Civilization* (Washington. D.C.: The Embassy of Saudi Arabia, n.d.), 8–9.

6. Ibid., 8.

7. Quoted in Franklin Graham, *The Name* (Nashville: Thomas Nelson, 2002), 71–72.

8. "Comparative Religions: Tough Questions and Easy Answers" (Toronto: Islamic Information & Da'wah Center International), accessed at www.islaminfo.com/articleview.asp?level=16&catID=1, October 16, 2002. Italics ours.

9. Islamic Affairs Department, *Islam: A Global Civilization*, 8.

10. Samuel P. Schlorff, *Understanding the Muslim Mindset* (Upper Darby, Pa.: Arab World Ministries, 1995), 31.

Chapter 5: The Godhead in Qur'anic and Biblical Thought

1. Samuel P. Schlorff, *Understanding the Muslim Mindset* (Upper Darby, Pa.: Arab World Ministries, 1995), 175.

2. Michael Sells, *Approaching the Qur'an* (Ashland, Ore.: White Cloud Press, 1999), 19.

3. Samuel M. Zwemer, *The Moslem Doctrine of God* (Boston: American Tract Society, 1905), 30.

4. Farid Esack, *On Being a Muslim* (Oxford: Oneworld, 1999), 19.

5. Al-Ghazali, *El Maksadu-l-asna,* quoted in Zwemer, *The Moslem Doctrine of God,* 31.

6. James Montgomery Boice, *An Expositional Commentary: The Gospel of John* (Grand Rapids: Baker, 1985), 1281.

7. A. Christian van Gorder, "Christians Meeting Muslims: Interfaith Discussions about the Nature of God" (Grantham, Pa.: Messiah College, n.d.), 38.

8. Ibid., 38–39.

9. Sells, *Approaching the Qur'an,* 19.

10. Aisha Brown, "Who Invented the Trinity?" The Institute of Islamic Information and Education Brochure Series: No. 22, accessed at www.uh.edu/campus/msa/trinity.html, October 22, 2002.

11. Ibid.

12. Ibid.

13. van Gorder, "Christians Meeting Muslims," 40.

14. *The Westminster Confession of Faith* (Atlanta: PCA Committee for Christian Education and Publications, 1990), 2.1, 2.3.

15. Sells, *Approaching the Qur'an,* 19.

16. van Gorder, "Christians Meeting Muslims," 38.

17. Esack, *On Being a Muslim,* 11–15.

18. Ibid., 19.

19. Samuel M. Zwemer, *The Moslem Doctrine of God* (Boston: American Tract Society, 1905), 120.

20. Esack, *On Being a Muslim,* 19.

21. Ibid., 29.

22. Ergun Mehmet Caner and Emir Fethi Caner, *Unveiling Islam* (Grand Rapids: Kregel, 2002), 104.

23. Samuel M. Zwemer, *Islam and the Cross* (Phillipsburg, N.J.: P&R Publishing, 2002, 153–54.

Chapter 6: Qur'anic and Biblical Living: Law and Grace

1. Islamic Affairs Department, *Islam: A Global Civilization* (Washington, D.C.: The Embassy of Saudi Arabia, n.d.), 9.

2. Michael Sells, *Approaching the Qur'an* (Ashland, Ore.: White Cloud Press, 1999), 14.

3. Dede Korkut, *Life Alert: The Medical Case of Muhammad* (Enumclaw, Wash.: WinePress Publishing, 2001), 108.

4. Yehia Sa'a, *All That the Prophets Have Spoken* (Durham, Ontario: GoodSeed International, 2001), 147.

5. R. C. Sproul, *Essential Truths of the Christian Faith* (Wheaton, Ill.: Tyndale House, 1992), 189.

6. Ibid., 123.

7. Ibid., 245.

8. Ibid., 255.

9. Sells, *Approaching the Qur'an*, 18.

10. Islamic Affairs Department, *Islam: A Global Civilization*, 9.

11. Sells, *Approaching the Qur'an*, 30.

12. *The Westminster Confession of Faith* (Atlanta: PCA Committee for Christian Education and Publications, 1990), 18.1.

13. Nancy R. Pearcey and Charles B. Thaxton, *The Soul of Science: Christian Faith and Natural Philosophy* (Wheaton, Ill.: Crossway, 1994), 21.

14. Korkut, *Life Alert*, 108–9.

15. Ibn Warraq, *Why I Am Not a Muslim* (Amherst, Mass.: Prometheus, 1995), 186.

16. Ibid., 172.

17. Ibid., 181.

18. Ibid., 187.

19. Christine A. Mallouhi, *Waging Peace on Islam* (Downers Grove, Ill.: InterVarsity Press, 2000), 343.

20. Arthur Bennett, ed., *The Valley of Vision: A Collection of Puritan Prayers and Devotions* (Edinburgh: Banner of Truth, 1975), 44.

Chapter 7: Communicating the Gospel of Grace to Muslims

1. Samuel M. Zwemer, *Islam and the Cross* (Phillipsburg, N.J.: P&R Publishing, 2002), 43.

2. Samuel M. Zwemer, *The Muslim Christ* (Edinburgh: Oliphant, Anderson & Ferrier, 1912), 183–85.

3. Fuoad Masri, "Muslim Extremists and the Great Commission," *World Christian* (December 2001): 46.

4. Zwemer, *Islam and the Cross*, 33.

5. James M. Boice and Paul S. Jones, "Come to the Waters," *Hymns for a Modern Reformation* (Philadelphia, TenthMusic, 2000), 21 (no. 7). Used by permission.

RESOURCES

BOOKS

Ali, Abdullah Yusuf. *The Qur'an*. Elmhurst, N.Y.: Tahrike Tarsile Qur'an, 2001.

Archer, Gleason L. *Encyclopedia of Bible Difficulties*. Grand Rapids: Zondervan, 1982.

Bahnsen, Greg L. *Always Ready: Directions for Defending the Faith*. Nacogdoches, Tex.: Covenant Media Foundation, 1996.

Bennett, Arthur, ed. *The Valley of Vision: A Collection of Puritan Prayers and Devotions*. Edinburgh: Banner of Truth, 1975.

Beverly, James A. *Understanding Islam*. Nashville: Thomas Nelson, 2001.

Boice, James Montgomery. *An Expositional Commentary: The Gospel of John*. Grand Rapids: Baker, 1985.

Caner, Ergun Mehmet, and Emir Fethi Caner. *Unveiling Islam*. Grand Rapids: Kregel, 2002.

Cleary, Thomas. *The Wisdom of the Prophet: Sayings of Muhammad*. Boston: Shambhala, 1994.

Coulter, Ian T. *Meetings for Better Understanding*. Philadelphia: Church Without Walls, 2002.

Crismier, Charles. *Renewing the Soul of America*. Richmond, Va.: Elijah, 2002.

Esack, Farid. *On Being a Muslim*. Oxford: Oneworld, 1999.

Geisler, Norman L., and Abdul Saleeb. *Answering Islam.* Grand Rapids: Baker, 1993.

Goodrick, Edward W., and John R. Kohlenberger III. *Zondervan NIV Exhaustive Concordance.* 2d ed. Grand Rapids: Zondervan, 1999.

Graham, Franklin. *The Name.* Nashville: Thomas Nelson, 2002.

Guinness, Os. *Time for Truth: Living Free in a World of Lies, Hype, and Spin.* Grand Rapids: Baker, 2000.

Islamic Affairs Department. *Islam: A Global Civilization.* Washington, D.C.: The Embassy of Saudi Arabia, n.d.

Korkut, Dede, *Life Alert: The Medical Case of Muhammad.* Enumclaw, Wash.: WinePress Publishing, 2001.

Lewis, C. S. *Mere Christianity.* New York: Simon & Schuster, 1943.

Lillback, Peter A. *Freedom's Holy Light.* Bryn Mawr, Pa.: The Providence Forum, 2000.

Mallouhi, Christine A. *Waging Peace on Islam.* Downers Grove, Ill.: InterVarsity Press, 2000.

Morey, Robert. *The Islamic Invasion.* Las Vegas: Christian Scholars Press, 1992.

Moucarry, Chawkat. *The Prophet and the Messiah.* Downers Grove, Ill.: InterVarsity Press, 2001.

Novak, Michael. *On Two Wings: Humble Faith and Common Sense at the American Founding.* San Francisco: Encounter, 2002.

Packer, J. I. *Knowing God.* Downers Grove, Ill.: InterVarsity Press, 1973.

Pearcey, Nancy R., and Charles B. Thaxton. *The Soul of Science: Christian Faith and Natural Philosophy.* Wheaton, Ill.: Crossway, 1994.

184

Reymond, Robert L. *Jesus, Divine Messiah*. Phillipsburg, N.J.: P&R Publishing, 1990.

Rosen, Moishe. *Y'shua*. Chicago: Moody Press, 1982.

Sa'a, Yehia. *All That the Prophets Have Spoken*. Durham, Ontario: GoodSeed International, 2001.

Safa, Reza F. *Inside Islam*. Lake Mary, Fla.: Charisma House, 1997.

Schlorff, Samuel P. *Understanding the Muslim Mindset*. Upper Darby, Pa.: Arab World Ministries, 1995.

Sells, Michael. *Approaching the Qur'an*. Ashland, Ore.: White Cloud Press, 1999.

Sproul, R. C. *Essential Truths of the Christian Faith*. Wheaton, Ill.: Tyndale House, 1992.

Warraq, Ibn. *Origins of the Koran: Classic Essays on Islam's Holy Book*. Amherst, Mass.: Prometheus, 1998.

———. *The Quest for the Historical Muhammad*. Amherst, Mass.: Prometheus, 2000.

———. *Why I Am Not a Muslim*. Amherst: Prometheus, 1995.

The Westminster Confession of Faith. Atlanta: PCA Committee for Christian Education and Publication, 1990.

Young, Edward J. *My Servants the Prophets*. Grand Rapids: Eerdmans, 1952.

Zaka, Anees. *Moslems and Christians: A Workbook*. Philadelphia: Church Without Walls/Biblical Institute for Islamic Studies, 2001.

Zwemer, Samuel M. *Islam and the Cross*. Phillipsburg, N.J.: P&R Publishing, 2002.

———. *The Moslem Doctrine of God*. Boston: American Tract Society, 1905.

———. *The Muslim Christ*. Edinburgh: Oliphant, Anderson & Ferrier, 1912.

185

ONLINE ARTICLES

al-Hanafi, Imam Ali Ibn al'Izz. "Evidences of Muhammad's Prophethood." Al Attique Publishers, 2000. Accessed at www.islaam.com/Article.asp?id=507, October 22, 2002.

an-Nawawi, Imam. "Prophet Muhammad's Miracles." Daar us-Sunnah Publications, 2001. Accessed at www.islaam.com/Article.asp?596, October 22, 2002.

Brown, Aisha. "Who Invented the Trinity?" The Institute of Islamic Information and Education Brochure Series: No. 22. Accessed at www.uh.edu/campus/msa/trinity.html, October 22, 2002.

"Comparative Religions: Jesus on Whom Be Peace in the Glorious Qur'an." Toronto: Islamic Information & Da'wah Center International. Accessed at www.islaminfo.com/articleview.asp?level=1&catID=1, October 16, 2002.

"Comparative Religions: Tough Questions and Easy Answers." Toronto: Islamic Information & Da'wah Center International. Accessed at www.islaminfo.com/articleview.asp?level=16&catID=1, October 16, 2002.

Khaliq, Shaykh 'Abdul Rahman 'Abdul. "Twelve Proofs That Muhammad Is a True Prophet." Originally published by IANA. Accessed at www.islaam.com/Article.asp:id=61, October 22, 2002.

Mohsen, Abdul Radhi Muhammad Abdul. "The Prophet Muhammad's Conduct and Morals as an Evidence of His Prophethood." IIPH, 1999. Accessed at www.islaam.com/Article.asp?id=424, October 22, 2002.

"More Info on Islam, Part 2." Accessed at www.angelfire.com/me/ummnurah/more.html, October 22, 2002.

"Priorities of Islamic Activities in the West." Shaykh 'Abdul Rahman 'Adbul Khaliq. Copyright Dar Ihyaa at-Turath. Accessed at www.islaam.com/ Article. asp?id=188, October 16, 2002.

PUBLISHED ARTICLES

Houssney, Georges. "The Arabs," *ReachOut* (June 1989).

———. "Arab Character," *ReachOut* (June 1989).

———. "Arabia in the Bible and the Qur'an," *ReachOut* (June 1989).

Masri, Fuoad. "Muslim Extremists and the Great Commission," *World Christian* (December 2001).

Schlorff, Samuel P. "Muslim Ideology and Christian Apologetics," *Missiology: An International Review* 21, no. 2 (1993).

UNPUBLISHED MATERIALS

"The Congressional Record and Bible Reading Notes." Immanuel Presbyterian Church, Norfolk. October 2002.

van Gorder, A. Christian, "Christians Meeting Muslims: Interfaith Discussions about the Nature of God." Grantham, Pa.: Messiah College, n.d.

INDEX OF BIBLICAL TEXTS

190

INDEX OF QUR'ANIC TEXTS

Anees Zaka (B.A., M.Div., a Middle Eastern university and seminary; Th.M., D.Min., Westminster Theological Seminary, Philadelphia; Ph.D., American University of Biblical Studies, Atlanta) is the founder and director of Church Without Walls (Presbyterian Church in America) and founder and president of Biblical Institute for Islamic Studies. Dr. Zaka has many years' experience in ministering to Muslims overseas and in North America. He has done extensive research on Islam for his masters and doctoral degrees and is co-author of *Muslims and Christians at the Table: Promoting Biblical Understanding among North American Muslims,* with Bruce A. McDowell.

Diane Coleman (B.S., Pennsylvania State University) has diverse working experience in several disciplines. She has served as a speech and language therapist, a program director for the profoundly handicapped, a biochemical research technician, and a curriculum coordinator and educator. She and her family lived in a predominantly Islamic country for several months. Her published works include a literary guide to the classic *Robin Hood,* two teaching manuals on phonics, and a privately commissioned company history entitled *It All Began with a Number Two Lead Pencil.*